On Christian Truth

On Christian Truth

What Christians Believe

Harry Blamires

REGENT COLLEGE PUBLISHING
Vancouver, British Columbia

On Christian Truth
Copyright © 1983 Harry Blamires
All rights reserved.

This edition published 2005 by Regent College Publishing
5800 University Boulevard, Vancouver, BC V6T 2E4 Canada
Web: www.regentpublishing.com
E-mail: info@regentpublishing.com

Views expressed in works published by Regent College Publishing are
those of the author and do not necessarily represent the official position
of Regent College <www.regent-college.edu>.

Library and Archives Canada Cataloguing in Publication

Blamires, Harry
    On Christian truth / Harry Blamires.

Previously published: Ann Arbor, Mich. : Servant
Books, 1983.
ISBN 1-57383-312-6

    1. Theology, Doctrinal—Popular works. I. Title.

BT77.B57 2005   230   C2004-901304-1

CONTENTS

Introduction / vii

One
Faith / 1

Two
The World Beyond / 5

Three
Everlasting Life / 11

Four
Soul and Body / 15

Five
Original Sin / 21

Six
Creation / 27

Seven
The Fall / 33

Eight
Providence / 39

Nine
God the Father / 45

Ten
God the Son / 49

Eleven
Jesus Our Savior / 53

Twelve
The Holy Spirit / 59

Thirteen
Unity in the Spirit / 63

Fourteen
Grace / 69

Fifteen
The Incarnation / 73

Sixteen
Evil / 77

Seventeen
God in Action / 81

Eighteen
The Crucifixion / 85

Nineteen
The Resurrection / 89

Twenty
Forgiveness / 93

Twenty-One
Love of God / 97

Twenty-Two
Love of Others / 103

Twenty-Three
Prayer / 107

Twenty-Four
The Church / 111

Twenty-Five
Suffering / 115

Twenty-Six
Joy / 119

Twenty-Seven
Worship / 123

Twenty-Eight
Revelation / 127

Twenty-Nine
Hope / 133

Thirty
The Christian Inheritance / 137

Introduction

THIS BOOK is a mixture of explanation and reflection. It seeks to explain, without jargon but with up-to-date examples, the meaning of some of the central articles of Christian belief. And it reflects on those beliefs in relation to our daily lives—our problems, our worries, and our joys.

The aim has been to give a lively account of Christian teaching, not shunning the grave or less grave objections which modern skeptics make to that teaching, but tackling them head-on. At the same time every endeavor has been made to keep the substance of the book self-explanatory. It is not dependent on the reader's familiarity with other people's thought. We hate it when we find ourselves in company where the talk continues a conversation that began long before we came to join it. Too many books of Christian guidance assume that readers are acquainted with recent controversies about doctrinal matters. This book makes no such assumption. After all, these controversies often detract attention from the crucial task of presenting Christian teaching plainly and squarely to those who genuinely want to know what it is. And that is what this book sets out to do.

Although the various sections tackle fundamentals, care has been taken to avoid what may be called the "rabbit-from-the-hat" approach. That is the approach which pretends to wipe the slate clean of all prior knowledge and eventually conjures the Christian faith, alive and kicking, out of a seemingly empty hat. "Let's assume that we know nothing of God. Here we are on this earth. Let's ask ourselves, What is the world for? How did it come to be?" If a writer begins like that when you know perfectly well that he believes in God and is a member of this or that church, you realize in advance what he is going to prove step by step, and the whole performance reeks of contrivance.

The reader will not find here any formal summary of metaphysical arguments for the existence of God. But he will find, I hope, a summary of Christian beliefs which at all points takes account of what people are thinking and saying and doing in the world around us, and does so without compromising logical or philosophical integrity.

ONE

Faith

MOST PEOPLE, if asked, would say that faith is the key to being a Christian. The unbeliever lacks faith, but the believer has it: that is what distinguishes him. And if this is generally accepted, then there might seem to be little to argue about in this first section. It might seem better to move straightaway to the really tough question: What is it that the believer has faith in?

But there are misleading notions about what having faith means. You will hear people talk as though faith is an extra piece of mental equipment possessed by Christians, enabling them to take for granted things which non-Christians would not accept for lack of reliable evidence. On this assumption, the man without faith can believe only in the existence of things like motor-buses and tadpoles, which can be taken to pieces and examined with the eyes and fingers, or in places like Chicago that can be visited any day you want, provided you have the money for the fare. The man *with* faith, however, can also believe in things like angels, who refuse to be examined in laboratories, and in places like heaven, which cannot be located on any map of the known universe.

Now this notion of faith is too simplistic by half. I have just opened a learned and authoritative textbook of the Christian Faith, and it says: "We ought not to believe the truth of any statement without evidence." That is as much a matter of common sense for Christians as for anyone else. Plainly, then, the idea of "faith" as a sort of admission ticket to the company of

1

those who accept a whole lot of things without proper evidence will not do. If faith is to be thought of as a special piece of personal equipment, it would be better regarded as something like a pair of spiritual binoculars. The mountainside across the way looks bare of living creatures. Pick up the binoculars, and you can spot a few climbers here and some sheep there. But neither climbers nor sheep are beings whose existence the man without binoculars would deny.

The whole notion of believing on inadequate evidence is alien to Christian thinking. The evidence for Christian faith lies in the Old Testament and the New Testament, the recorded life and teaching of Jesus Christ and the apostles, the witness of saints and martyrs through the centuries, and the personal experience represented by every book of Christian prayers or exhortation or testimony ever written. Such material can scarcely be dismissed as too flimsy or insubstantial to support a reasoned case.

Believing by faith, then, is not the opposite of believing by evidence, though it may be accepted that much of the evidence accepted by Christians in support of their faith is different from the evidence studied by scientists for purposes of investigation. For that matter much of the evidence accepted by historians for the purpose of arriving at the truth is also very different from the evidence studied by scientists in laboratories. When we turn to judge the historical evidence of the gospel story and the truth of Christianity we must be careful not to apply different yardsticks from those by which we form our other notions of historic truth. The yardsticks which some skeptics apply to the evidence of the Christian revelation, if generally applied, would bring into question the existence of Julius Caesar and the conquests of Napoleon.

Just as it is wrong to think of faith as a matter of believing without evidence, so also it is wrong to think of faith as being opposed to reason. The idea that faith and reason are opposite methods of arriving at illumination is quite wrong. You have just read a page and a half of reasoning about the character of faith. If you persist to the end of the book you are going to read another hundred pages and more of reasoning about the character and substance of faith. The interdependence of faith and reason is inescapable for men and women to whom God has given minds.

Faith, then, is not an isolated faculty which certain lucky people just happen to possess. It is not a kind of spiritual credit card randomly distributed. (If you've got one, you can go along to the divine autobank, tap out your request in prayer, and collect the wherewithal to keep you going. If you *haven't* got one, too bad.) Yet popular use of the word "faith" often conjures up the notion of something you acquire or lose by sheer chance. Someone writes in his or her autobiography, "At the age of twenty-six I lost my faith." Perhaps it is one in a sequence of misfortunes. "At the age of ten I lost my mother." "At the age of eighteen I lost my virginity." "At the age of twenty-five I lost my passport." "At the age of forty I lost my teeth." "At the age of fifty I lost my hair."

"I lost my faith." My passport too. And while my passport had enabled me to travel the world on pleasure or business, my faith had enabled me to traverse large tracts of thought and communication now suddenly closed to me. One day I could board a plane for Europe, and the next day they wouldn't let me through to the departure lounge. One day I could talk to God, confess my sins, pray for my friends, revel in the deeds of Moses and Elijah, rejoice in the teaching of St. John and St. Paul. And the next day it was all gone. The whole fabric had collapsed, vanished. It was now nonexistent.

It is absurd to regard faith thus as the ticket to an otherworldly region of thought and contemplation which can be withdrawn, cancelled, or lost in a flash. Nevertheless the passport and the gift of faith do have *one* thing in common. If you lose either, you alone are the loser. International airlines continue to operate even though you can no longer travel on them. And neither the history of Israel, nor the gospel revelation, nor the long chronicle of the Church's life and growth will evaporate when you lose your faith.

Suppose you met a man who said, "Shortly after his

reelection I lost my faith in President Nixon." What would this tell you? Would it cast doubt on Mr. Nixon's continuing existence after that date? Did the speaker now have to question whether the President still lived, still ran an administration? Did he say to other people: "Yes, I have lost my faith in the President. There is no such place as the White House. It is the fabrication of wishful thinking. It is part of a dream-world which has no credible connection with real men and women living their daily lives"?

We should ponder the close connection between "faith" in a public figure or a great teacher and faith in God. Faith is trust. The greater the faith, the greater the trust. The more total the faith, the more complete is the personal commitment to the individual believed in. That aspect of the Christian's faith is the most crucial aspect, because it is the thing which drives missionaries and saints to heroic deeds of self-sacrifice for the God they believe in.

But who would pretend that the beginner will necessarily have a rich faith in this sense? Yes, there may be cases where he can. But more likely the person who is just turning to the Christian community in the hope of finding the Christian God and the Christian Way is going to need months or years of spiritual nourishment and discipline before he or she can evidence faith in that kind of fullness.

So what kind of faith is asked of the beginner? In a sense, faith in other people's faith. He must recognize that apostles like Peter and Paul believed and were transformed. He must remember that there were many suffering people whom the Lord himself touched and healed, and to whom he said, "Thy faith hath made thee whole." He must note that all around in the living Christian community of today are men and women professing that same faith, and he must be ready to try what it is like being one of them.

TWO

The World Beyond

YOU CANNOT SAY a single prayer without coming down heavily on one side of a great barrier—the barrier that separates those whose minds accept that God exists from those who would deny our right to make such an assumption. So reason is involved in the first act of faith. Reason allows that there *could* be a God; otherwise faith could never say, "There is, and I trust him." Reason starts the process by saying something like this: "There *must* be Someone at the back of this extraordinary thing that we call human history, lived through in this remarkable corner of the vast universe."

Someone at the back of it all, someone who started it all off, someone who actually made the thing as a craftsman makes something with his hands, someone who thought it all up as a writer thinks up a play or an inventor devises a new machine.

"And why?" asks the atheist, "do you need to invent a God in order to explain the existence of the universe? Isn't it all self-explanatory? This world has manufactured itself by a process of evolution, and we men and women are the products of the process—apparently the best and perhaps the final products. Nature has produced you and me just as she has produced jellyfish and volcanoes."

Now there is a very odd thing about our first reply to the atheist in this matter. We don't say, "No, I can't allow that." We say, "But wait a minute. That's the whole problem. Nature has produced me in so far as I am flesh and blood, brains and

5

nerves. Nature has produced every living being. Why is it that (and *how* is it that) Nature has managed to produce a race of beings who have minds that ask, 'What's behind it all?' How can natural evolution, as we understand it, throw up creatures who turn on natural evolution and say, 'You're not adequate to account for me. There's something behind you'? The trouble (the trouble for the atheist, I mean) is that it's not *unnatural* to believe in a God or gods. History suggests that it's the most natural thing in the world. It seems to demand a highly developed brain to conceive of a causeless universe that manufactured itself. Commonsense hankers after a cause for everything, a maker of everything, and some kind of purpose behind everything.

So there is this great divide between those people who think that the universe we experience with our senses and study with our instruments is the be-all and end-all, and those who believe there is something more than that, something indeed surer, more lasting, more purposeful than that. We must not think that this great divide simply separates Christians from non-Christians, for of course it separates all believers in divine beings from all who are convinced that the universe does not allow for them. The latter can properly be called "naturalists." Their creed is "Naturalism," the belief that the world of time and space is the whole show, the belief that there is no life except the life of growth to death within the natural order.

Those who refuse to accept that the natural order is the whole show and insist that, at the very minimum, there is at least one being who was not born as you and I were born and will not die as you and I will die, can justly be called "supernaturalists." They believe that there is something above (super) Nature and, in that sense, their creed is some kind of "supernaturalism."

Christianity is of course a religion of the supernatural in that Christians reject the idea that the running-down world of time and space is the only reality, and that the life lived between cradle and grave is the only life ever to be experienced.

"Supernatural" is an easily misunderstood word. It tends to

be used popularly of what are called paranormal phenomena. It conjures up in people's minds ideas of ghosts, mediums, table-tapping, poltergeists, and the like. This is a pity. There is a perfectly good word for such phenomena. They are "preter-natural"—that is to say, outside the apparent laws of the natural but not necessarily *above* them, and therefore not superior to the natural order in the way that the things of God may be superior. It would be better if Christians kept the word "supernatural" for the things of God, and used the word "preternatural" for seemingly non-natural manifestations that have nothing to do with genuine religion. Perhaps it would be better still if we also used the word "sub-natural" (*below* the natural) for non-natural manifestations that originate with powers lower, and not higher, than mankind.

Now some people new to the Christian faith are apt to assume that the most crucial aspects of Christianity are its supernatural aspects. They recall how pagans worshipped the sun and moon, and how primitive peoples regarded trees and rivers, thunder and lightning, and all kinds of natural objects and events as gods and goddesses. And they tend to think, "Christianity has got beyond all that. Its God is spiritual. Earlier religions were crude and earthbound. Christianity lifts us above all that."

These are half-truths. It would be wrong to think of the development of religion as being itself a kind of evolutionary process, to assume that crude primitive belief which sees magic all around in the living world gives way to a more and more denaturalized faith whose emphasis is on things spiritual. The most remarkable thing about Christianity is indeed that it is *not* simply a supernatural religion. On the contrary, it claims that God, who is the maker of all things, is also the God who came to earth, lived a human life, and died a human death. Christianity is therefore a very remarkable religion indeed. In the first place it says, "There is a state of being beyond time and space where God dwells eternally." But it does *not* go on to say, "So this life here in the natural order is not all that important. It is peripheral. It must be counted a trivial, ephemeral experience that passes away like a dream." No, instead of that, Christianity goes on to say, "But this world of space and time has been visited by God himself. He became one of us. He demonstrated indeed that our passing physical life here can be involved with his eternal life beyond and above the universe."

And this is one reason why the history of Christianity has been a history of controversy and division, of fierce arguments and cruel struggles. Because a religion which demands a balance between its supernatural and its natural aspects is always capable of being misinterpreted, first in one direction, then in the other. There will always be Christians who say, quite rightly, "Our God lives in eternity and calls us to spiritual communion with what is deathless and timeless," but then, unfortunately, go on to say, "So we must not distract ourselves from the main business of religion, which is prayer and worship and sanctification. We must not fuss over the passing needs of the world around us." And, on the other side, there will always be Christians who say, quite rightly, "But our God came to earth, helped and healed the troubled, sanctified the life of the body by being one of us," and then, unfortunately, go on to say, "So we must not distract ourselves from the main business of religion, which is to comfort and aid our fellowmen. We must not fuss over the minutiae of worship and the cultivation of our own souls."

The conflict represented, rather crudely, by these alternative emphases, runs through Christian history. There is hardly a quarrel in the long story of Christendom that is not in some way a struggle between the competing claims of the supernatural emphasis and the natural emphasis of Christian teaching. The issue is with us today. And anyone who joins a church, of whatever denomination, will encounter it in some form. It may come before him in some highly abstruse doctrinal form in argument about how far Christ was God and how far he was a man. Or it may come in some more immediately practical form in argument about whether it is the Church's job, in some seemingly dire crisis, to forgo the work of evangelism and throw its resources into support of some cause that will bring physical and material benefit to deprived and exploited fellow-creatures.

Mainstream Christianity always holds the two seemingly competing emphases in balance.

THREE

Everlasting Life

THERE IS A GREAT DEAL in the Bible and in Christian teaching about "everlasting life." I suspect that there are lots of people who, if they were asked, "What is it that these Christians believe?" might say something like this in reply, "Oh, they hold that this life is not the only one, and that when we die we shall move on to another one."

Well, of course, this statement is not false; but it is terribly inadequate. And, like many things said about Christianity by uninformed people, it can be so misleading that it can do as much damage as a direct falsehood.

For if the main difference between Christians and unbelievers were that Christians have an additional life in prospect at the end of this one, then the crucial quarrel between Christians and others would be about the distant future and not about the immediate present. The atheist would be able to say to the Christian, "Well, you have this belief in a future life. I don't accept it, but you have the right to hold it. And fortunately it does not prevent us from jogging along happily together in this present life—which we both believe in."

But in fact the Christian teaching about everlasting life is not just teaching about the future; it is teaching about the present. And all we have said about natural life and supernatural life would be misunderstood if they were thought to be two kinds of life that man can experience in turn. To put the error crudely: There is God up there in the supernatural world, with the angels (if there are such things), and men and women who have lived on earth in the past; and here are we in the natural realm, and, if we conduct ourselves here as we ought, there will eventually be a place for us up there alongside them.

Every great Christian saint and teacher has insisted that this life here and now has to be different for the believer than for the unbeliever. The "difference" is *not* that the Christian is always congratulating himself by saying, "Thank God there is something more after all this eating and sleeping, getting ill and dying; thank God there is something else as well as these buildings that will one day crumble and this earth that will one day be burnt to ash!" For this "something more" and "something else" do not have that kind of separateness from what we experience here and now. It is pagan to hold that we are part and parcel here of a physical structure that will vanish totally into nothingness. Rather this life is different for the believer than for the unbeliever in that the believer is always saying to himself, "This experience of looking at trees that will die and climbing mountains that will crumble, this experience of loving a wife and having children who are all destined eventually for the grave, is inextricably mixed up with an order of things that cannot pass away. God's kingdom is eternal, and it interpenetrates this natural world so that at any moment the leaf of a tree, the light in an eye, or the sunset on the hills may speak of its wonder."

In short, the Christian inhabits two worlds at once. Or, if that is putting it too strongly for most of us, the Christian saint inhabits two worlds at once, while the run-of-the-mill Christian like ourselves inhabits one world while time after time catching glimpses or picking up hints of what lies behind and above it.

It cannot be too strongly emphasized that to become a Christian is to accept an extra dimension to life. From the Christian's point of view the notable thing about the unbeliever's world is that it is much *smaller* than his. Indeed, from the Christian's point of view, the unbeliever is imprisoned in a decaying universe. He has locked himself in.

Imagine that a not-very-intelligent child were taken to the theater to see some tragedy like, say, *Hamlet,* at the end of which the stage is littered with corpses. And suppose that you had some difficulty in comforting the child after the performance, so distressed was he at the spectacle of the deaths. "But the man who played Hamlet is not really dead," you explain. "He is an actor. Not only does he perform these parts on the stage, pretending to be a Prince of Denmark or some other such imaginary character, he also lives a life outside the theater. He has a wife and family and, far from being dead, he has probably now gone home to them to enjoy a late supper."

It is difficult for the Christian writer to know how far he ought to go in pressing this parallel. He runs the risk of sounding arrogant and conceited. For the unbeliever, looking out on the world, is really like the unintelligent child who takes the play for reality and fails to sense that the actors and actresses are ordinary men and women. If there is one word which the Christian secretly wants to use time after time to describe the narrowness of the unbeliever's outlook, it is the word "literal." To look out on the world and fail to sense its Creator's hand is really due to that massive deficiency of imagination which we call "literalness": not seeing the forest for the trees.

Put like that, it sounds disgustingly smug. Out there are a lot of poor benighted unbelievers, and here are we in the Church, let into the secret of God's mysteries. Up to a point we have the right to feel cheerful about this distinction. There is an awful lot in the New Testament about living in the joy of the resurrection, which is tantamount to finding delight in the gift of everlasting life. But there is a converse to all this. The gift of eternal life, the merest fragmentary hint of the divine hand at work around us or the divine eye watching over us brings a double unsettlement.

The first unsettlement consists in realizing how far adrift from God the world has shifted. Yes, unbelievers *are* benighted; they *are* missing out on what is most crucial to happiness, and indeed to understanding of the world they live in. But how numerous they are! And how greatly they seem to be in the ascendant! How widely they influence the thinking of their fellowmen! It may be joy to the Christian to feel that, however dimly and faintly, he has at least touched the heart of the matter in acknowledging God's lordship and the power of the redemption, but the *greater,* the surer his Christian confidence in this respect, the more worryingly horrific is the spectacle of millions of fellow-beings trying to cut themselves off from reality.

That is the first unsettlement, which could all but dowse Christian joy in the cold facts of contemporary life. Our contemporaries, by and large, are ignorant of God. They don't want to hear about him. It has been said that our age has lost the taste for God and that today man prefers himself. When such thoughts hit the mind of the Christian, can he dismiss them while he goes on rejoicing in the gift of everlasting life?

And, as if this disquiet were not enough, there is a second unsettlement. The greater our sense of being blessed in the faith, the more tragic the alienation of our contemporaries seems. And the vaster this alienation, the more absurdly inadequate we feel to do anything at all that is worth doing. The greatest gift in the world has been given us. The refusal of most of humanity to want it for themselves is our first distress. Our inability to do anything to touch them in this respect is our second distress.

One might well conclude that the gift of faith is a doubtful blessing indeed. If joy there is, well and good. But it is accompanied by such disquiet that we are tempted to feel that it might have been more comfortable for us to forgo the joy and thereby escape the consequent disquiets.

So does the believer sometimes envy the unbeliever? Fleetingly, yes. In the same way that the learned scholar, tussling with some taxing problem, might look up from his book, catch sight of an unlettered gardener at work in his garden and fleetingly wish that his problems were no subtler nor more obdurate than the gardener's. In the same way that the boss of a big business, worrying over complex financial or managerial problems, might look out of his office window, catch sight of office-cleaners clocking in for work, and momentarily wish that his duties could be as readily and untaxingly performed as theirs.

FOUR

Soul and Body

I CAN IMAGINE A READER who might now be getting impatient and saying to himself: "I picked up this book in order to find out something more about Christianity. It's a religion of love; I know that. It's all about brotherhood and helping others. It's supposed to bring us together in one great, happy human family. But judging from what I am reading here, Christianity doesn't do anything of the kind. It seems to mark all believers off from the rest of us. They live in a different mental world, it appears. How can they bring harmony to quarrelsome humanity? They are at loggerheads with most of their fellow-men."

I'm afraid they are. Perhaps the worst misconception of the Christian message is that which represents it as a soothing syrup, a dose of which will magically transform you into everybody's chum. If you commit yourself to our Lord Jesus Christ you will certainly find yourself at home in the company of fellow-believers, but the mass of our contemporaries are not fellow-believers, and you will find yourself in new ways separated from them.

"But surely," my questioner protests, "there is nothing fundamentally divisive about one man believing in everlasting life and another man not believing it. You say the first man has got the bigger, grander notion of the human being's role in things; but he's not going in a different direction from the second man, is he? And when the second man dies he will learn in the next life, if there is one, what he has not learned in this

15

one. Christian belief in the immortality of the soul is something
that applies to all people, isn't it?"

Now in fact this book has said nothing at all about the
"immortality of the soul." The belief that we human beings are
made up of two distinct constituents, a body that will be buried
or burnt at death and a separable soul that will survive it is not
strictly a part of biblical teaching. It was a pagan Greek notion
that each man has an indestructible component carried about in
an obsolescent body. Built-in immortality is not a specifically
Christian concept. When one talks about "everlasting life," one
is talking about something that God gives, not something that
man automatically has. We have to be very careful here, because
we have been told that it is not our business to judge. It is God's
business to judge. No Christian has the right to declare all who
are officially "unbelievers" lost to eternity. But every Christian
needs to make biblical teaching clear—if only to himself. And
the barrier between believers and unbelievers does not divide
those who know that man has everlasting life from those who do
not know—and therefore must be informed. It divides those
who *have* everlasting life from those who (at present) have not.
And straightaway, having made the point clear, one must rush
in with qualifications. The New Testament is full of warnings
about what may be in store for people who think themselves
righteous and presume to call familiarly upon our Lord. And it
is full of reminders that apparent outsiders may come flooding
into the kingdom of heaven at God's call while those who
believed they had a right to be there find themselves locked out.

Here I detect a new disquiet in my reader. "I took up this
book," he says, "because I wanted to learn about the Christian
idea of God. I'm seeking some assurance that the Prime Mover,
the Creator of the universe—whatever you want to call him—is
really in charge and really cares. And already you have
introduced fanciful stuff about a future life of bliss in heaven.
It's too soon for the beginner to start calculating his chances of
acquiring wings and a harp. Frankly I'm not very interested in
that prospect anyway. Can't we put first things first."

But the odd thing is that, when the apostles and early

disciples set about the task of spreading the gospel across the world, this was in fact the first thing they stressed, the great new truth. They preached the resurrection. And they preached the call to repentance. The forgiveness of sins and the resurrection of the body: this was the message that built up the early Church.

The two doctrines are inextricably linked together. Perhaps one ought never to talk about the resurrection of the body until one has talked about the forgiveness of sins. But here the need is to distinguish Christian belief in the resurrection of the body from pagan belief in the immortality of the soul. And we shall not get the thing clear if we approach it with a Greek notion of the distinction between body and soul, between the doomed physical thing and the undying spiritual thing. The word "body," as now used, is itself likely to confuse us. Christian teaching does not offer us eternal existence as disembodied "spirits" but as complete persons. For eternal life is not life from which all the richness that we know through the senses and the brain is creamed off. It is this life *plus*.

We do not lack experience to indicate what this might mean. St. Paul uses the parallel of the seed and the flower. The seed, in a sense, "dies." It is buried. But what grows from it was contained within it from the beginning. The mystery of growth is all about us in the natural world. We recognize it as "given," part of the scheme of things. Sunshine and shower play their part, but the mystery remains. Christian teachers have often used the example of the way a caterpillar becomes a chrysalis and then a butterfly to illustrate the way a hidden potential for transformation to new life may be realized through a process of apparent "death." Certainly, if we allow at all for the idea of a Creator of our universe, we must accept that one capable of devising such processes as these would have no difficulty in transforming our earthly beings, through death, into heavenly beings. And of course one might add that the kind of God who concocted the one idea might well concoct the other. Indeed, since this principle of growth through burial seems to be crucial to the natural scheme of things of which we are a part, it is logical enough to assume that we ourselves partake of it.

One of our difficulties today is that we have got into the habit of sectionalizing everything. We mentally split things up into their component parts. We have got to do so when we think about machines. If your car won't start, you have to locate the fault in the ignition, the plugs, the carburetor, the petrol pump, or whatever. And we quite properly think of a car as the assemblage of all its parts. Indeed we know that it was constructed piece by piece on an assembly line. But men and women are not assembly-line products. No one worked in a factory piecing organs together, stitching flesh to skeleton, and sewing the whole thing up in a bag of skin. It is true that, within a limited sphere, engineering work can be done nowadays on defective sections of the body and "new" parts fitted from discarded models. But the human being, grown from egg and seed and foetus, is plainly more like a flower in construction than like a motor-bicycle. There are things you can take to pieces and reassemble, and things you can't.

But because of our mechanical-mindedness we tend to picture the human being as a collection of components. This habit even extends outside the purely physical sphere. Man's mental machinery gets sectionalized into ego and id and libido, and the rest of it. In educational institutions you will find tutors filling up forms which call for students' abilities and qualities to be summed up under headings like: "1. Initiative; 2. Imagination; 3. Resourcefulness; 4. Perseverance; 5. Self-Criticism; 6. Open-mindedness." One student has a big 3 and a small 6, a lot of 1 but a lack of 4. A bit of skilled engineering by his tutors, however, can turn him into a better all-round product. The counsellor takes out his psychological tool-kit and soon has him tuned up.

We are not made like that. And we must not twist Christian teaching into such a shape that it supplies an extra component to an otherwise adequately functioning mechanism. The "soul" as that indestructible black box which will be flung out of my frame when it finally crashes, and will contain tape recordings of all my doings for the delectation of my companions in eternity—that idea will not do.

We are complete personalities. The Christian promise of eternal fulfillment is not a piecemeal arrangement for special little bits of us. This is one way in which the Christian doctrine of the resurrection of the body differs from pagan doctrines of the immortality of the soul. And there is a second great difference between these teachings. The assumed immortality of the soul is a built-in attribute. Man has it by definition. But the resurrection of the body is the special gift of God. Man does not in his own right have it. Indeed, he has forfeited all due title to it. But that is another story.

FIVE

Original Sin

CHRISTIANITY TEACHES that man is a "fallen" being. Some people speak of this as a "pessimistic" doctrine. But it is not so. They say that Christianity takes a poor view of human nature. But this is not true either. If you visited a school where discipline was slack, where lessons could not proceed smoothly because the children were racketing about, fighting with each other, and damaging the equipment, you would come away saying: "That's a poor school. The pupils are getting nowhere." And suppose the headmaster heard this and said: "What a cynic you are. It's quite unjust to denigrate education like that. If you have so little faith in schools and children, you're no help to the young. I'm an optimist myself. I happen to believe in the young, and I've no time for pessimists." What would you make of that? How would you wish to reply? Surely you would wish to say: "But it's precisely because I *do* believe in education that I think poorly of your school. It's precisely because I *do* believe in children and in what they can achieve that I am distressed to see them behaving as they do here."

Which of you really believes in the young and in education, you or the headmaster? Which of you is the more inclined to cynicism and pessimism—the headmaster who thinks that there is no more to be expected of children than is evidenced in a bear-garden, or you who expect to see a well-regulated school where the pupils study and learn?

The Church's doctrine of Original Sin says, in effect, that something has gone wrong with human nature so that it is not functioning as it ought. As it *ought*. Man is not behaving in accordance with the true requirements of his own nature. He is letting himself down, as we say. You have to have a generous estimate of what being a man or a woman is all about if you are going to insist that, generally speaking, we are all letting ourselves down badly. In this sense the doctrine of Original Sin is an optimistic doctrine. Man's true nature, it says, is one thing, and his observable conduct is a very different thing. I believe it was G.K. Chesterton who said it would be more accurate to call the doctrine of Original Sin the doctrine of "Original Innocence" because it insists on the integrity and uprightness that was proper to humanity in its unfallen condition.

Have there been periods of history in which the doctrine of Original Sin might have seemed implausible and difficult to defend? Have there been times when intelligent men and women could say to each other: "But there is no evidence of any widespread rot in the civilization we live in. By and large people are working hard, living soberly, bringing up their children to be upright, honest, and industrious. Everywhere in our society we can see more and more help given to the poor and afflicted. There is progress in health-care, education, culture, and all the things that make for the good life. One cannot speak of human nature as 'fallen' when the evidence is that we are gradually building a just and humane society living in peace and prosperity"?

Certainly the Christian today is not likely to be confronted by that objection. The optimistic humanists of the early days of our century, who taught that a bit of intelligent social engineering and a dose of psychological liberation would soon rid us of poverty, crime, and misery, are not much in evidence today. Our countries are wracked with crime and corruption even though ever greater provisions have been made for the education and welfare of our peoples. Crime, vandalism, and terrorism increase year by year. We can scarcely believe that it is not forty years since the President of the United States could take a daily walk in Washington along the streets surrounding the White House. When I was a boy there were no areas of the large industrial city I was brought up in that were closed to us by day or night. When we went to the theater we walked back home three or four miles through the center of the city to the suburbs in the late hours as cheerfully and as securely as in the daytime.

It needs no elaborate argument today to establish that men and women do not behave as they ought; that there is some kind of tendency at work in their bloodstreams pulling them toward evil. That is half the meaning of the doctrine of Original Sin: man has an ingrown tendency to evil. The other half of the doctrine's meaning is that this ingrown tendency is not a true characteristic of human nature but a perversion of human nature. Man was made innocent and somehow "fell" into corruption. Man was intended to be one thing and turned out to be another thing. Every healthy instinct and intuition in us recognizes that this is true. We are "torn" beings, divided creatures, wanting to make a perfect world and succeeding in making a perfect mess of things. It is true of humanity in the large. It is true of you and me in our individual lives.

All sin is disobedience to God. Whatever man was created for, he was certainly not created to run a world in which millions die of starvation in one country while millions live in luxury in another, a world where any man might get stabbed any night for the sake of his wallet, where governments pile up unspeakable weapons capable of poisoning whole nations and turning their cities to ash. We know in our hearts that this is not how it was meant to be. The God who made us gave us those hearts and that knowledge too. In short, we recognize our sinfulness, our disobedience to God. We may not, as individuals, have played seemingly any great part in the decisions and developments that have produced the major public ills around us. But we all contribute our daily bit of pride and selfishness to the fund of evil that in aggregate produces the gigantic human rebellion represented by the modern world.

The Christian message speaks of the forgiveness of sins. Could any message be more relevant to our condition? If we do not sense the blessing of that message as a spiritual kiss of life, then surely we are numb from head to toe, insensitive beyond recovery. The man who can look out on the twentieth-century human scene in our countries and not long for the grace of forgiveness upon himself and his fellowmen has either no imagination or no morality.

Our Lord Jesus Christ has won forgiveness for us. That is what the Cross was all about. And that is what his resurrection established. He rose from the dead and men thereafter rushed about the world proclaiming not only the conquest of death (which was obvious in the risen body), but also the conquest of sin. They announced that a new humanity was now available. The old one was corrupt: that was as obvious then as it is today. But God's originally created humanity having proved faulty, he was now offering a re-designed version, road-tested in the severest conditions. The original model was being recalled as defective and a substitute with a new maker's guarantee put on the market and made freely available to anyone who was ready to trade in the old model for the new. When you try to put it into new imagery, the imagery will always seem laughably inadequate in many respects. But there was no doubt what the message was. As the first man of the Old Testament story, Adam, had been led into sin, and had thus introduced a spreading strain of infectious evil into the human bloodstream, so the first man of the New Testament revelation, Jesus Christ, had somehow disinfected humanity of its corrosive disease and injected the pure blood of a new creation into human veins. The blood-transfusion is on offer to all.

Why, then, is there as much evil about us as ever? Because the offer of a blood-transfusion is not taken up. That is to say, it is not taken up by humanity at large. Men and women of the old creation live alongside men and women who claim to accept the new creation. Perhaps it is not surprising that people so difficult to be stirred that they cannot get excited about the conquest of death and the offer of eternal life will also shrug off the conquest of sin and the offer of a newly minted humanity. But no man of sense and sensitivity can pretend that these tremendous offers are irrelevant to modern man's needs. Every daily newspaper, every daily news bulletin, every other shop-window, every other utterance by the media, proclaims the rottenness of unregenerate humanity and the desperate need of the world for forgiveness and new life.

SIX

Creation

WHEN SOMEONE ASKS A QUESTION beginning with the word "Why" it generally means that, as we say, he wants to get to the bottom of things in some respect. He sees something and he wants to trace it back to its origin or its purpose. When my child asks, "Why is that man standing there by that lamp-post?" I reply, "Because it's a bus stop. The bus driver halts there when he sees someone waiting, and the man will be able to get on." The child is satisfied. At the bottom of things in this instance is a man who intends to catch a bus and that intention accounts for what he is doing.

The human intention is not always so directly traceable. I am going to put up a new shelf in the kitchen and my child asks, "Why are there two holes in that bracket?" I reply, "So that I can screw it firmly to the wall. If it had only one hole, you see, it could easily be moved. It needs two to make it firm." Now in this case you can scarcely say that my intention to make the shelf firm is the full explanation of the two holes. Even the child knows that. He wouldn't put it into words, but he has accepted that somewhere along the line of cause and effect behind this bracket there was a designer who knew what was needed to keep a shelf firm and who drew a diagram to guide the workmen who manufactured the bracket. Once more the question has been answered by tracking down the human intention at the bottom of things.

It is so natural to us to think in terms of intention or purpose

27

that we keep the game up even when, strictly speaking, *human* intention is not involved.

For instance, I am a townsman born and bred, and now that I live in the country I have to ask lots of questions of this kind. We put food out for the birds in winter just in front of the kitchen window. The robins and chaffinches are there in a flash, the blackbirds soon after. But how slow the bigger birds are. The gulls wheel around for ages before they decide that it's safe to land in the garden. They then frighten off the smaller birds who have hitherto seemed so much braver than they. As for the magpies, they keep their distance while we are watching at the window. If we withdraw into the shadow of the room hunger may drive them down, but the slightest visible movement on our part drives them off.

I comment on this to my wife who knows all about such things. "Why should those big birds be so timid and neurotic while the little ones are so bold and tame?" And she explains. "The little ones can get away quickly in an emergency and they are too small to be easy targets anyway. The gulls need taking-off space. Unless they can see a runway that is long enough they are hesitant to come down. The hedges here and the wall of the house make this piece of ground rather too enclosed for them. The magpies, of course, are at a worse disadvantage still. They are heavy and clumsy. Taking off is for them a comparatively laborious business. Besides, their coloring makes them so conspicuous. They are the easiest targets of all."

I am satisfied with this explanation. Or am I? What have we got to at the bottom of all this? A chaffinch who thinks, "Tee hee, I'm small and light and swift. It's safe enough for me to go after those bread-crumbs"? A gull who measures the runway and questions whether it's long enough for a swift take-off in an emergency? A magpie who reflects, "Phew! With my sluggish acceleration from starting and with my white stripe flashing in the sunlight I wouldn't have an earthly if one of those two in the kitchen is carrying a loaded gun"?

This is not what satisfies me. I have only the vaguest notions of how intelligent birds and beasts are. I gather that they have something called "instinct" which we can refer to when we want to explain why an animal does something for which there is no explanation. Being a skeptical person myself, I have always assumed that "It does that by instinct" is just the technical way of saying, "I don't know why it does that."

What does satisfy me is that the explanations given me have traced the birds' behavior back to an intention, a purpose. When we have tracked down that purpose in the natural world we are happy. The hedgehog has spikes so that it can roll itself into a ball and present a pretty unpalatable mouthful to a hungry marauder. The rabbit stands stock still so that it can be mistaken for a stone, a piece of wood or foliage, and the eyes of the game-keeper will pass over it. The coloring of the squirrel enables it to fade invisibly into its background. These are certainly not animal purposes in the sense that there was human purpose behind the design of the shelf-bracket. Even if you argue that the hedgehog is in some way aware of its unpalatability as a ball of spikes, you cannot argue that animal-intention devised the spikes. And we are certainly not dealing with human intentions. Indeed we are speaking of an intentions-system, or a collection of purposes, that applies to the human as well as to the animal world.

Why have I got two legs? So that I can walk. Why have I got two eyes? So that I can see. Why have I got two hands? So that I can pick things up and feed myself.

From day to day, from hour to hour, we think of the natural world we live in as being directed by an overall purpose that is more basic than human purpose could ever be. It is the biggest lie of bogus learning to pretend that cold commonsense is against the idea of a universe designed and overseen by a divine Creator.

What is the alternative to belief in a divine Creator?

There used to be a theory that evolution could explain everything; it has always been suspect to philosophers and theologians, but it is now under fire from scientists themselves. For this reason: that if you eliminate the idea of divine purpose you have no other logical alternative than to believe that the universe we know has developed by accident. On this principle all our thinking which traces events back to intentions or purposes is invalidated. Ever since science began we have been wrong to ask "Why this?" and "Why that?" if "Why?" seeks to uncover an intention, a purpose; for there is ultimately *no* intention, *no* purpose.

This does not mean that all evolutionary science is mistaken. On the contrary, it has wonderful things to tell us about the development of the natural world. But if I answered my child's question, "Why are there two holes in that bracket?" by giving a thorough and detailed account of how the metal was made and the bracket manufactured, I should not have answered his basic question. He would have acquired a large amount of useful knowledge, yet his basic curiosity would remain unsatisfied. And it is precisely such knowledge of the universe that science supplies.

Evolutionary science as an investigation of the natural order is illuminating. Evolutionary thinking as an explanation of what the world is all about is totally absurd.

You can often test a theory by translating it into cruder terms. You can clarify a theory about the universe and its making by finding a human parallel. And it is logical enough to think of a universe created on the principles of invention and design that are present in human projects. To think of God as the great clock-manufacturer who not only put the machine together but also wound it up is crude and inadequate but *not in all respects totally absurd*. Consider the evolutionary principle by contrast. Take it and imagine its human parallel. One day a movement of the earth threw up a row of stones here and a row there. Another day a flood left them covered with mud. The sunshine hardened it. There were more and more disturbances of the earth's surface, more floods, more stones and mud till one day the piled-up stones had become walls. Trees were split by lightning and fell on top of them. Winds carried branches and deposited them above. Pieces of slate, splintered by earthquakes from mountain-sides, came flying in whirlwinds to land on top. By degrees we can thus trace how this house we now live in came to be. Human purpose, human design was not necessary. Natural forces, over millions of years, pieced it together.

That is how you think and that is the kind of thing you believe if you accept mindless evolution as a way of accounting for the world we live in.

The Christian believes in a God who thought it all up and brought it into being. And he gave it the kind of overall consistency that makes exploration of its various parts always exciting and illuminating. He made us men and women too. And we were made in his image. Which means that, like him, we can think in terms of design and purpose. We can, in our small way, mimic his art of devising and fashioning what is useful and beautiful. We can, in our small way, track down through the study of this bird or this rock, that planet or that galaxy, those principles of interconnection, of harmony, of design, which evidence his guiding hand.

SEVEN

The Fall

THIS IS THE POINT FOR THE CYNIC to ask an obvious question: If a good God made the world and all that is in it, why did he make such a mess of it? A God capable of conceiving and manufacturing the galaxies and inventing the molecular structure of material things clearly has consummate resources at his disposal. It surely ought not to have been beyond his wit to produce a race of beings on earth whose history was something better than a record of cruelty and greed, injustice and despoliation.

We can argue about God's purposes and his doings only by taking a look at man's purposes and doings, and then projecting them on to the cosmic scale. When we speak of God "making" the world, we project thoughts about making houses or motorcars, statues or poems, on a massive screen. We magnify the familiar into the gigantic. It is our only method of reasoning about matters which are, essentially, too vast for our minds to conceive.

And if you consider the things that human beings make, you will notice that the more complex and subtle they are, the more easily can they "go wrong." The more wonderful they are, the finer in conception and execution, the simpler it is to pervert or deface them. I doubt whether human minds could conceive of a world in which this principle did not apply: the principle of correlation between increasing complexity and increasing openness to perversion. For instance, if a child takes his black ink and daubs a mark on a rough table he is working at, the table could in

33

no sense be described as ruined. But if he were to apply the same treatment to Titian's Venus of Urbino and give her a moustache, he would literally ruin a masterpiece. He may carve his initials on a school desk with his penknife and no great harm is done. But if he is found trying to chisel them on the flanks of the Venus de Milo he will be in deep trouble.

The same principle applies to our mechanical "creations." The ignition system of a car depends on a complex set of engineering calculations and on a finely measured system of "timing." A minor defect in the distributor can spoil the car's performance and even bring it to a halt. A typewriter is less complex and subtle in design than a telephone system. If you press a single wrong key on a typewriter you may or may not make your message uninterpretable. The reader of a typescript has no difficulty with "box of trickx." If, like me, you happen to have fingers that regularly misrepresent "unclear" as "nuclear" and "true" as "ture" you may confuse some readers, but the context will probably clear the matter up for a discerning reader. But if you press the telephone keys in the wrong order you can end up communicating with someone in Hong Kong instead of someone in New York. The one thing that is certain is that you will not get in touch with the person you wanted. The effect of a typing slip may be cancelled out by human understanding. The ill effect of a dialling slip on the phone cannot.

The world of music can supply especially apt exemplification of this principle. An organ which has dozens of stops and thousands of pipes requires only that one or two such pipes should cipher (sound when they are not supposed to) and the instrument becomes virtually unusable. The organ is an example of complexity of design. The violin might stand as an example of fineness and subtlety of design. A slight maladjustment of one of the pegs that holds the strings in place puts the instrument out of tune with potentially disastrous results. Consider what complexity of fine tuning and fine timing goes into the performance of a single Beethoven symphony by a full orchestra. One willful trombone player, inserting a note wrongly here and there, could totally devastate a performance.

The principle that the finer and more complex the creation, the more susceptible it is to ruinously perverse misuse has been explored here but has not been "explained"—in the sense of "accounted for." I don't know whether it can be accounted for. (There was a time when professional philosophers used to try to explain such matters. But now few of them concern themselves with real life issues; they are too busy concentrating on the meaning of words. Real life issues will have to wait until they have decided that they have got a reliable verbal equipment for dealing with them.) The only world we know is the world in which this principle operates. And therefore we ought not to be surprised that men and women, the most subtly and complexly and finely created things in the world of our experience, should manifest the same principle, and manifest it very clearly. God made them with a physical, mental, and spiritual equipment capable of such fine tuning that they could themselves build cathedrals, write epics, and invent space vehicles, but he refused to program their achievements. Everything else in the world might be in some degree programmed, but not men and women, because they were made in his image. They were to be themselves programmers, not computers.

This is where the parallel between divine creation and human creation breaks down. Beethoven, the creator, writes his symphony. He gathers his orchestra together and distributes the parts. They learn them. They discipline themselves to play exactly the notes written for them; nothing more, nothing less. We have been speaking as though we men and women were like orchestral players who have to keep our instruments in tune and play our parts with perfect coordination. But God did not give us this soft option in life—that you should keep your fiddle in tune and I should keep my flute in tune; that we should both play the prescribed notes in the right order and contribute to a harmonious performance of a neatly orchestrated full score. There is no full score. God did not choose to manufacture a race of string-players and wind-players in due proportion. He seems not to have wanted a lot of well-trained instrumentalists.

Instead he wanted us all to be Beethovens, and he scattered the potential for that as widely as human seed is scattered.

This is only another way of saying that God decided to create a race of beings like himself. The risk involved in this, the rashness of it, is surely breathtaking. If we were all, as it were, instrumentalists who had been given our parts to play, then the possibilities of a total universal fiasco would surely have been reduced. One or two of us might play out of tune here and there, miscount the rests and come in at the wrong time, lose our place in a movement, or have a fit of coughing or giggling in the middle of a pianissimo, and yet the overall performance might still be recognized as a genuine, if shoddily performed, symphony. But making us a lot of Beethovens, a lot of creators, ruled out for us this possibility of somewhat mediocre ventures into shabbiness and inadequacy. For the result of God's decision is that we have all got our own tunes in our heads, we all want to persuade others to join in, learn our score, and keep time to our beat. The potential for artistic disaster built into this scheme is mountainous.

When reflected upon, God's preference for a race of potential Beethovens instead of trained and accomplished instrumentalists was surely the height of rashness and folly. The world's telephone system was cited as an instance of something so complex that the least slip of a finger could set a bell ringing in Tokyo when it was meant to ring in London. God gave men and women minds each one no less complex than such a world system, and then he threw in freedom as an extra ingredient too. It was as though, having netted the world together telephonically, the super engineer of the whole had said, "We'll scrap fixed links between dialling codes and numbers, and the lists set out in the telephone directory. We'll substitute a random principle that allows every subscriber to make his own relationships through imaginative use of numbers."

Sometimes one wonders whether there is after all anything remarkable in the fact that human beings have made a hash of things in so many ages and in so many respects. Given their equipment and given their freedom, isn't it perhaps more astonishing that they should ever have risen to the building of civilizations, the spread of scholarship, the organized care of their less fortunate fellow-creatures? Does man's tendency to evil after all require explanation? We Christians, recognizing that a good God made the world and all that is in it, including ourselves, feel it necessary to explain to the rest of humanity how evil has come to be. Man was created good, but he fell. That is one way of putting the human dilemma. Man was created free, but he managed to discipline himself to the practice of virtue and the construction of a civilized order. That is an alternative way of putting the human dilemma.

Man was not programmed, yet he sometimes produced the right answer. Man was not given a schedule, yet he sometimes did the right thing at the right time. Man was not coerced, yet he learned to use language and tools to make poems and space-shuttles. What a wonderful benign Providence must have watched over him!

The fall of man; and the rise of man: how can anyone dwell upon the one without dwelling upon the other too?

EIGHT

Providence

WE USE THE WORDS "providence" and "providential" care-lessly. "It was providential that I got to the station early because they had re-timed the train to depart ten minutes sooner." The word slips out naturally. "It was providential." And perhaps we don't mean exactly the same thing as we would mean by, "It was sheer good luck." In our minds "luck" describes the wholly fortuitous event, the coincidence that randomness sometimes throws up—as when someone proves to have the winning number in a sweepstake. But when we say "providential" we convey the faintest sense of something other than pure chance at work. There is the slight hint of a beneficent purpose operative somewhere at the back of things.

The most familiar objection to the Christian faith is expressed by the question, "How can you believe in a good God when there is so much evil in the world?" I sometimes wonder why we don't more often hear the question, "How can you deny that there is a good God when there is so much good in the world?" The very fact that we are by nature tempted to ask the first question and not the second question is *in itself* a kind of proof of divine providence. For it shows that we are surprised, not by good, but by evil. No amount of goodness in human beings causes us to ask deep philosophical questions about our life in the world. But when we encounter a streak of real evil we have to "explain it away." No amount of goodness in the given world sets us questioning the ultimate nature of things. But a single disaster makes us cry out, "Why? Why?"

39

The sun can shine daily, ripening the corn, and no explanation seems to be called for. A single flash of lightning kills a man and we feel immediately that someone "up top" ought to explain himself.

Is it possible to conceive of a person in this world whose upbringing and experience were such that his or her mind worked in the opposite way? Might there have been, say, a little Jewish girl who grew from infancy to childhood in Belsen, taking in enough to sense the total hostility of the "Powers that be" to all goodness, all love, and all delight? And at the end of the war the child was taken to the west to find herself in a country where the "Powers that be" seemed to want her not to suffer and indeed seemed to lack the accustomed preference for cruelty and destruction. Might she perhaps feel that this remarkable aberration required some special explanation? The poet Dryden has a brilliant phrase about a foolish man who "never deviates into sense." Might our little girl feel that the novel human deviation into goodness required some accounting for?

I think not. I do not believe that even such a child could ever find goodness worrisomely odd. It would rather bring a sense of relief, of escape from unnaturalness into naturalness. I do not believe that any experience of sustained and vicious ill-treatment succeeded by sudden generosity could ever leave a person asking, "How can I accustom myself to this extraordinary phenomenon of human decency?" The human response to goodness could never be, "What is all this about?" It would always be, "At last! This is what life should be like."

The sense of "Providence"—of an overriding goodness at the base and heart of whoever or whatever governs the universe—seems to be a built-in feature of human nature. If it were not so, why should any of us make a fuss about the prevalence of evil? If there is no good Providence, why should anything ever go right? If there is no good Providence, why should we feel that evil has to be especially accounted for? If there is no positive purpose behind the international telephone system, why should I ever get through to the person whose number I have culled from a book and dialled?

The Christian believes that God created the universe and, by his good providence, sustains it and watches lovingly over its inhabitants. He has watched so lovingly that when those inhabitants strayed into evil he sent his Son to save them. The freedom he gave them made it possible for them to stray into evil just as it made it possible for them to be makers and initiators like himself.

How does God's watchful providence work? It is easy to mock the notion of a God who sits in an office feverishly trying to keep up with individual human requests accumulating in his In-tray. Mrs. G. prays that her husband may be cured of cancer and Mr. Y. prays that his wife may conquer her alcoholism. These, and millions more, are worthy requests. Indeed they chime in with God's own wishes. He would like to see Mr. G. happy and healthy, and he deeply desires that Mrs. Y. should keep sober. Why, then, does it transpire that Mr. G.'s cancer proves to be terminal and that Mrs. Y.'s addiction gets worse?

We cannot pretend that there are slick answers to these questions. Nevertheless they certainly do not bring the fact of divine Providence into question. The complex tangle of human affairs is such that sometimes a good result can be achieved only out of what is in itself "evil." Cancer is plainly an evil in that it eats into the health of bodies given to us by God. Mrs. G.'s prayer for her husband coincides with God's own wish that men and women should enjoy the life he has given them. On the other hand, it is a mortal life. Everyone must die sooner or later. And from a divine point of view perhaps Mr. G.'s death at this point is going to be fruitful. Perhaps Mr. G.'s son has lost his faith. Perhaps the shock of his father's death will bring him back on his knees in prayer again.

A God who was capable of devising the universe and making men and women is certainly capable of seeing all round events which to us seem separable from the overall pattern of human doings, but which in his eyes are knit together. God is our father. We are his children. Even at the human level all parents know that it is not always good to answer a child's request, even though it is a worthy request and for his sake we would dearly love to answer it.

Suppose you have two sons. John is six and Jim is four. Jim, the younger, is rather more assertive and pushful than his elder brother. He is inspired with the natural desire to catch up with his big brother, John. He wants to do everything his elder brother does and, if possible, do it better. The elder brother, John, is good-natured, reticent, and gentle. Jim is now almost as tall as he is. You see the risk that John may shrink back into his shell if this young brother Jim too clamantly monopolizes the attention of others. One day you take Jim out while John is at school. Jim sees a picture-book in a shop. He wants it badly. It is a good book. You want him to have it too. You approve of his wish to romp away at reading. But Jim is already almost catching his brother up in this respect too. He asks you to buy him the book and, gently, you refuse. Jim is disappointed, and perhaps a little bewildered. He knows that you like to see him read. He knows that books are a very good thing in your eyes. And he was feeling rather proud of himself for having asked for a book instead of for a comic or a bar of chocolate. You see eye to eye with Jim in all these respects and you are sad to have to rebuff him. Yet you persist in doing so. Why?

In your mind you are seeing something which Jim cannot see. You are picturing what will happen after you return home. John will come home from school. Like any child who has recently started school he will naturally be sensitive to the fact that his younger brother or sister has spent the day in the bosom of the family and has possibly gained ground somehow as a result. You want to forestall the kind of possible psychological development that might occur if John is welcomed at the door by Jim excitedly pushing the new book in his face and saying triumphantly, "Look what Mummy has bought me!"

Now some of my readers, parents or non-parents, may exercise their ingenuity in providing Mummy with other ways of solving the problem than refusing Jim his book. She can buy

Jim his book, they might say, and buy another one at the same time for John too. But Mummy has in fact considered this possibility and rejected it. She knows that Jim's triumphant flourish of his new book could not be fully balanced by her saying, "And I've bought one for you too, John." To begin with the book will not be John's own choice. He may not fancy it. And anyway John is intelligent enough to sense that this second purchase has been made in order to put him on a level with his own younger brother, Jim. Indeed Mummy's determination to give Jim what he wanted has been so strong that she has parted with money too in a blind effort to comfort John, and John is not absolutely sure that he wants to be comforted on those terms. . . .

(I could go on. For the number of complex and moral psychological matters weighed by Mummy during those few moments in the shop make her husband's business problems of the day as company executive seem trivially untaxing on the brain by comparison. When it comes to responsibility for priority-selection and decision-making most top executives and administrators could probably learn something from Mummy— including a few home-truths about why flight from house-bound motherhood to a top professional job is often an escape from tackling what is important and imaginatively taxing to dealing with what is comparatively trivial and mechanical.)

God's good providence is certainly not brought into question by this or that instance of a prayer apparently unanswered. If we were to press the parallel of the little parable we have used, we should point out that Mummy's love for her children is equal. Her love for Jim seems to require one act: her love for John seems to require another act. Her "providence" operates in this instance by denying Jim's "prayer" even though she thoroughly sympathizes with its intention.

God's love for his children and his concern for their well-being cannot be less demanding than that of a human parent. The complex interrelationship of psychological need on the part of the various children in a small human family can tax the wisdom of the parents. The vast network of interrelated human needs present to God's mind as prayers reach him from this member and that member of his massive family will certainly give him a vastly different perspective on those requests from what is present in the minds of those who pray.

NINE

God the Father

GOD IS NOT ONLY CREATOR of all things and overseer of all things, he is our Father. Perhaps it is necessary to clear the air over the use of the masculine noun, "Father." Objections to it as "sexist" are red herrings. I once attended a meeting of a college academic board where the chairman took up, as the next matter on the agenda, a new scheme proposed for controlling time-table schedules. We all studied the relevant papers and the chairman asked, "Who fathered this plan?" "I did," said a female member of staff, and no one thought it sounded odd. Later in the meeting, when we had turned to more immediate personal matters, the case of a student came up who had suffered a bereavement and one or two other personal troubles, and she was clearly in need of special attention. The chairman looked around the room after her case had been aired. "Well," he said, "who's going to mother her?" A male member of staff immediately replied, "I will. I know her very well." Again no one thought it sounded odd. Both words, "father" and "mother," can be used in such detachment from their sexual connotations that a woman can "father" something and a man can "mother" someone.

God might be thought to have taken a great risk in making human beings in his own image. Indeed it involved granting them such a degree of free choice that they were able to upset the whole apple-cart of creation. But, being made in his image, we can at least dimly understand the impulse that moved him. Human parents have heard the phrase that to have children is "to give hostages to fortune." What is meant by the expression is that the joys of parenthood and the worries of parenthood, if one were to make a balance-sheet of the two, might together show a heavy deficit. Indeed there is always the possibility of a quite crippling grief caused by the misfortune or misbehavior of a son or daughter that can virtually bankrupt a parent of peace and happiness. Even without any such major disaster the parental profit-and-loss account will be a chequered one. Father and mother may delight in every stage of baby's progress to childhood. There are moments, however, in the middle of the night or in the early hours, when baby begins to scream for the fourth time and they wonder what madness seized them to father and mother the irrepressible brat. But on the whole the smiles next day, the stumbling first steps, the halting first words, the clutching and clinging hands soon wipe their doubts away.

If you are a parent you know all about this. At all stages Grandma and Grandpa warn you that "the worst is to come." They assure you that there is no point at which the parent can say, "Now I've finished. The job is done. The worry is over." To begin with there are the physical perils besetting all of us—the risk that a child will be knocked down by a car, attacked by a criminal, or afflicted with some dreadful disease. What blows these can be. Do you personally know a parent whose son or daughter will never walk again, never see again, never speak again?

And yet, heavy as these griefs can be, there are heavier burdens for parents still. And they do not necessarily decrease as childhood gives way to adolescence and to youthful maturity. The problems of managing teenagers can be far more devastating than those of handling infants. Mr. and Mrs. A. have had to watch their son turn into a heroin addict. Mr. and Mrs. B. have had to watch their daughter turn into a call-girl. Mr. and Mrs. C. have seen their son convicted of robbery with violence. Mr. and Mrs. D. have seen their daughter rounded up with a bunch of terrorists.

Do these parents wish they had never had children? Do they

not rather wish that their children had turned out differently? Are they likely to say, "If only one of us had been infertile!"? Are they not more likely to exclaim, "If only we had acted otherwise at this or that stage in bringing up John or Joan!"? Are they likely to say to couples just entering on marriage, "Whatever you do, don't have any children"? Are they not rather more inclined to give positive advice: "If you have children, make sure that you give them plenty of affection and not too much independence too soon"?

Suppose someone put the question to them: Would you rather that your children had never been born or that they had turned out more to your liking? Surely they would choose the second alternative.

That is why I think Thomas Hardy was wrong when he wrote a poem ("By the Earth's Corpse") in which God repents that he ever made the world and its creatures. Human history has been such a tale of wrongs that, when life is at last extinct and the earth grown cold, God grieves over his mistake in creating them. There is surely something sterile in this way of thinking, and one wonders whether Hardy might have written differently if he had not himself been childless. As a father, he might have reflected less regretfully on the making of free beings. When we have experienced and understood the terrible risks of parenthood, we can begin to grasp what God's fatherhood means. We can glimpse its appalling potential costliness. And we can appreciate how understandable it was that God should mount a rescue operation for his human family so painful and so cataclysmic that all time and eternity reverberate under its impact.

God sent his only-begotten Son, our savior Jesus Christ. His mission was to offer brotherly union with himself in a restored, recovered sonship-daughtership, sins forgiven and a new start made. The human race needed this second chance because by and large they had opted out of God's family. The human race was a generation of drop-outs. They had gone their own ways, falling for this addiction and for that, joining a network of subversives, and plotting an alternative society. For God's established society had rules and regulations laid down by the prophets of old. Murder, covetousness, theft, adultery, idolatry, and other such self-centered acts were proscribed. And the subversives, then as now, would brook no inhibitions. They wanted a society in which everyone could do his own thing. They wanted to turn "obedience" into a dirty word. This was and is the alternative code which has inspired the growth of terrorist cells in all ages, the binding of men and women together with high-sounding phrases for the purpose of undermining God's rule. The history of the human race has in heaven's eyes been a history of guerilla activity, sniping here, planting a bomb there—a massive campaign of furtive destruction.

What does the guerilla campaign consist in? Every act of willful selfishness and pride that asserts the individual against the law of God. You and I are involved in it today, just as the cruel and wicked enemies of God's people and the despoilers of his temple were involved in it in Old Testament and New Testament times.

God sent his Son to call us home. "Come out of that underground movement, return to your loving Father, and all will be forgiven. Forsake that sinister band of rebels. Turn your back on their specious chatter about human rights. There are no human rights. There are only human duties."

God sent his Son into a world overrun by subversive forces. He was bound to be taken hostage. And, just as every parent knows that his children are "hostages to fortune," so God knew that his Son was now hostage in the hands of subversives. The subversives killed their hostage: but God raised him up from death and, from that moment, the ultimate defeat of human subversion was assured. For the power of subversives is the power of the bullet and the bomb, of terror and blackmail. Bullet and bomb deal death. Terror and blackmail trade in fear of death. When death is itself conquered, the last weapon, the indispensable tool of subversion is destroyed. When God in man was raised from the dead, the human rebellion was drained of its resources.

TEN

God the Son

FEW THINKING PEOPLE TODAY would dispute that the human race has made rather a mess of things. What many of them would jib at is the Christian claim that God has mounted a rescue operation. Oh yes, they would agree that a rescue operation *is needed*: indeed they are forever planning their own rescue operations, striving to put things right by increased education, by increased welfare services, by human rights campaigns, and, in very dire emergencies, by costly wars undertaken to defeat tyranny and injustice. Yet, in so many respects, things get worse instead of better. The ironical stage is reached at which the main agency of our human rescue operation—our schools and colleges—become themselves infected with the evils they are designed to eradicate from the larger world. Have we fully faced up to this development? That institutions established to civilize are becoming breeding-grounds of barbarism? Can we look the facts in the face without realizing that no human rescue operation is going to work? The divine rescue operation is our only hope.

When men and women come to appreciate that only a divine rescue operation could save the human race, they might justifiably throw up their hands in despair, were it not that for two thousand years a body of people has insisted that a divine rescue operation has in fact been mounted and that its saving power is available to all.

God sent his Son to recall his people to their senses. They killed him. God made his death at their hands the epitome and consummation of all human sinfulness, all human rebellion; then cancelled it out by raising him from the dead. There are a dozen ways of explaining this marvel and none of them is adequate. Words like "sacrifice," "atonement," and "ransom" are used to try to clarify the mystery. But mystery it remains. The Son shared the humanity of God's earthly children, partook voluntarily and unresistingly of their most dreaded experience, death, then rose again to life. And what made this miraculous event so world-shaking was that throughout his ministry the Son had offered men and women a share in his life, membership of his very body, common sonship-daughtership of his Father. All this he offered to them under the terms of a new dispensation which made death acceptable and resurrection its outcome.

When a prophet appears, miraculously healing the sick and restoring the dead to life, people will naturally heed him. When that prophet declares himself the Son of God and, indeed, one with his Father, they will take note that the claim fits in with his supernatural powers. When he tells them that he can forgive sins and bring them the gift of everlasting life, they may feel that the message is too good to be true. And when he is arrested, flogged, nailed to a cross, and killed, they may reasonably assume that that is the end of the matter. But when he rises from the dead on the third day, appears to many, and galvanizes his body of followers into what turns out to be a worldwide campaign for belief in his authority and power, then they can no longer resist his call and his promise.

For the call and the promise, then as now, chime in with every healthy commonsense response to the world about us. We can see that man has failed in his own power. We cannot but believe that man was meant to be good and happy. In our best moments we cannot ourselves think except in terms of putting right what has gone wrong. Whoever made us so that we think like that will surely himself want to put right what has gone wrong.

Because God is not just our ruler but our Father, the disobedience of the human race could not be dealt with by punishment and correction, by intervention which compelled men to a change of course. Such compulsion was, as we say, "not on." It is not on for human parents. God no more wants mechanical, reluctant "obedience" than human parents want it. The true father does not want an obedience bred of fear or a chill sense of duty. He seeks love; the love that will certainly express itself in obedience where it is appropriate. Punishing and correcting disobedient children is one thing. Restoring them to a free relationship of loving obedience is another thing. That is why talk about Christ paying off man's debt to God is a little too cold and clinical. That is why we have teachers who speak of human sinfulness as something which makes a chasm between God and ourselves. And they speak of Jesus Christ as throwing himself into the gulf yawning between us.

It is odd that, in some respects, modern life gives new vitality to stories and parables which had come to seem remote. The story of Adam and Eve, for instance, at first sight seems distant from our life and environment today. Adam and Eve, God's first human children, are placed in a beautiful home, supplied with all the good things needful to a happy and prosperous life. Yet they throw it all away through failure to obey a single injunction. The one thing they are forbidden to do, they do. In short, there is that streak of willfulness in them which must be satisfied. It is not enough for them to have the good things of life; they must also have their own way. And not having their own way in one single respect so transforms their outlook on the good things they *have* got that they are ready to put them all at risk. So they opt for independence. They are the first drop-outs.

We ought not to have difficulty with a story which cuts so near the bone of contemporary life. Is it not the sons and daughters of well-to-do business and professional men, young people surrounded with the good things of life who, in sheer willfulness, opt out and join the subversives? One must not pretend that in all cases the parallel is a just one. No doubt our drop-outs contain many unselfish idealists who in conscience reject the setup which distributes wealth and privilege so unjustly. But there is a core of truth and illumination in the parallel. Adam and Eve turned their backs on their loving

Father, chose to disobey his sole injunction—the one rule that indicated their dependent status. In them and through them the human race dropped out.

Intermediaries were sent to call them home. The prophets reiterated the wickedness of their rebellion. But nothing served. God had to send his only Son to wipe out the effect of their disobedience in his own self-sacrifice and to offer restoration to faithful human sonship in brotherhood with him.

Let us put it another way. The human race is aboard a hijacked jet flying through time. God himself directed its takeoff from the divine control-tower. The initiator of all evil, whom we call the Devil, managed to get a boarding-pass. When cruising height was reached, he produced his weapons, threatened the pilot, and took control of the jumbo and all its passengers. So it hopped on uncomfortably through history from airport to airport till it was caught on the tarmac at Jerusalem, an outpost of the Roman empire, in the reign of Tiberius Caesar, where the Son of God offered himself as sole hostage in exchange for passengers and crew. The further you push the parallel the more fanciful it seems. But the basic idea of the human race aboard a hijacked jumbo flying through time is sound enough. The passengers must keep a wary eye on the hijacker, induce the pilot to take his directions from God's control-tower, and be ready to accept rescue through the sacrifice of the willing Hostage. That is their only escape route.

ELEVEN

Jesus Our Savior

W HEN YOU COME TO THINK ABOUT IT, quite a lot of our talk about God in the last few sections has been somewhat presumptuous. We have said that he made the world, that the project went wrong, that he mounted a rescue operation for the fallen human race, and so on. We have observed how his divine Providence is exercised over human affairs. We have pictured how he deals with the volume of prayer that reaches him. Notice what we have been doing in talking like this. We have been looking at the world and at human history with a God's-eye-view. We have been looking down on the world and on the human race and trying to sum up the events of centuries as only a divine being above space and time could sum them up.

Can a being like a man, a unit among millions on a single planet which is a microscopic dot in the unimaginable reaches of the universe, reasonably expect to get the secret of cosmic things taped so that he can begin to talk about the purpose and descry the meaning of the whole created order? Is his worm's-eye view likely to match in any respect the view of an eye that overlooks the galaxies?

When you turn up a large stone on the ground to bring to light a colony of ants scurrying about their business, you are suddenly reminded that a whole world of life and activity can exist on a scale far far smaller than the scale of our own daily experience. You certainly get something that matches a God's-eye view when you look down on the ant world. If your eyesight were sharp enough, you could begin to discern a vast complexity of busy activity by hundreds of creatures. But how would that same situation strike an individual ant among those hundreds? Clearly no single ant could watch the movements of hundreds of others and take in the total picture as you take it in. The ant certainly does not observe its own ant-world as you observe it. Quite apart from this limitation of the ant-view, there is presumably an even more drastic limitation in the ant's response to the lifting of the stone. For the stone is not to the ant-consciousness what it is to yours. Its movement, affected by the force of your foot, knocks the roof off the ant-world. Can we imagine anything like it in our own experience? If the sky above our heads were suddenly cut away to be replaced by a vast emptiness quivering with an intolerably blinding light, no doubt we should all scurry for shelter.

We would not wish the ant, if it is intelligent enough, to be deprived of the right to speculate about what had happened when the stone moved and the blinding light shattered the frame of its world, but clearly it would have immense difficulty in shifting from an ant's-eye view to a man's-eye view. If there were an ant with a record-breaking I.Q., which really gave its mind to the matter, we can perhaps imagine the way it might explain to itself what had happened. For ants themselves shift bits of earth, and our brainy ant, if it could conceive of a creature thousands of times bigger than itself shifting a piece of material thousands of time bigger than the pieces it could shift, perhaps for the purpose of building a home thousands of times bigger than its own nest, then it might perhaps begin to understand. It might ask itself, "Who moved the stone?"

Of course there is one situation in which ants might really be shaken out of their rather limited ant-perspectives. And that would occur if a man managed to transform himself temporarily into an ant, to come to work alongside them and try to convert them to the man's-eye view of their doings and their world.

Let us, for a moment, stop trying to achieve the God's-eye view. Let us forget the great drama of creation and redemption worked out by the divine playwright, and humbly file back into our individual roles in the massive cast. Let the great stone block off our view of heaven as though no hand or foot had ever rolled it away. Let us look only with human eyes and hear only with human ears, even though sometimes it is through the eyes and ears of others. What has happened under this great stone of sky?

A child was born in Bethlehem and his name was Jesus. When he grew up he healed the sick and restored the dead to life. He called himself the Son of God and declared, "I and the Father are one." He called men and women to repentance and exhorted them to have faith in him. He gathered a small group of disciples around him and hinted to them that he must die and be raised from the dead. He broke bread and blessed wine for them, declaring that in partaking of it they were feeding on his own body and drinking of his own blood. Shortly afterwards he was killed, but then rose from the dead. And his disciples carried his message across the world.

That is what human eyes and ears witnessed. There is no God's-eye view in that. There is just the testimony of men and women who had neither axe to grind nor material product to sell. It is the testimony of men and women who in many cases laid down their lives rather than deny what they or their predecessors had seen and heard of Jesus, the Son of God.

And what is there for human eyes and ears to witness today— apart from this record of what happened long ago?

There is the testimony of millions of men and women of all races and of all ranks, of all varieties of accomplishment, and of all levels of understanding, that they have found in a person, Jesus Christ, a savior, a brother, a friend, who has lifted the burden of guilt from their hearts and given them peace and stability.

Do not, if you are an unbeliever, if you are skeptical, be put off by the fact that this experience seems to mean a thousand different things to a thousand different people. In one man the heart and core of it seems to consist in a vocation of personal evangelism rooted and grounded in expounding passages of the Bible. In another man the heart and core of it seems to consist in regular attendance at Mass, regular confession to a priest, and the thumbing of beads in prayer. Do not make the mistake of thinking that these two men are involved in essentially different systems of belief. For both of them devotion to their savior Jesus Christ is the living center of their practice and their convictions. Indeed the variety of modes in which Christian devotion to Christ manifests itself is a strength rather than a weakness of the Christian religion. G.K. Chesterton told how he had been compulsively drawn to Christ by the fact that he was a person whom everybody praised for a different reason.

As we read the Bible and the works of wise Christian teachers, a hundred Christs pass before our eyes. There is Christ the King and Christ the carpenter of Nazareth. There is the Son of God seated at the right hand of the Father in Heaven and the child of Mary lying in a manger. There is the Good Shepherd and the true Vine, the Spouse of the Church and its cornerstone, the Sower of seed and the Fisher of men. Christ is the high priest standing at the altar and the servant with water and a towel kneeling at your feet. He is the Light of the world and the Knocker at your door. He is the Lamb sent to slaughter and the promised Messiah.

It is not surprising that those who claim to serve him can do so in fashions so diverse.

But so far as your first encounter with him (and mine) is concerned, he is simply the Savior, offering us the forgiveness of our sins and the hope of everlasting life. And around him cluster the multitudes who tell us, "Yes, it works. Stop failing on your own. Stop trying to succeed on your own. Take him for what he is, God's own Son. And ask him to take you over."

For conversion is a spiritual takeover. Jesus Christ is God's own broker buying up shares in human hearts, hoping to corner that fifty-one percent holding in your heart and mine that will pull one more going concern into the divine portfolio. For having scattered shares in happiness throughout the world by giving freedom to all men and women, God has set himself the task of building up a monopoly of human hearts from scratch without any leverage. As shareholders we are free to sell or not to sell, and he is trying to buy into each one of us. With such a purchaser in the field, the shareholder who knows a good thing when he sees it will not hesitate to sign away his full holding. For this is a take-over with a difference. The divine operator plays the market only for the profit of those he would buy out.

By degrees we have slipped back again into trying to attain the God's-eye view. Forget the divine Broker raiding the earthly stock-exchange. Remember how it looks, and looked, down here. Remember the Savior with the human face moving towards the cross.

TWELVE

The Holy Spirit

WHAT DID I FIND when I turned up a textbook of theology for an account of the Holy Spirit, or the Holy Ghost? The first thing I found was this:

> God the Holy Ghost is the Third Person of the Blessed Trinity, equal to God the Father and God the Son, and of one essence with Them.

Now there is no doubt that here we have the God's-eye view. There they are, all Three of Them, Father, Son, and Holy Ghost, united in a Blessed Trinity, seated in eternity, raised aloft above our little universe as it sails through time with the human race aboard.

I'm not sure that this picture helps you and me much. I'm not surprised when the text books tell us that the doctrine of the Trinity "is not explicitly stated in Scripture, but has been worked out by the Church as the only possible conclusion from the evidence given in Scripture." For on the whole the New Testament tells us things we can understand without taking our eyes from the earthly scene.

What about a man's-eye view of the Holy Spirit?

Jesus promised his disciples that he would send a Comforter to them "from the Father" himself. He assured them that the Holy Spirit would come upon them, and from the Spirit they would receive power enabling them to be his witnesses throughout the world. This was the promise. And it began to be realized on the day of Pentecost when the disciples were gathered together in a house. Suddenly there was the sound of rushing wind, and over the head of each of them there appeared a tongue of flame. "And they were all filled with the Holy Ghost." That was the beginning. And the sequel was that the apostles were changed men. Courageous, wise, overflowing with enthusiasm, they embarked on the task of converting the world.

That is the man's-eye view of the Holy Spirit recorded in the New Testament. What of the man's-eye view of the Holy Spirit today?

You will not find people walking about with flames above their heads, though bishops still wear headgear ("mitres") shaped like cloven tongues of flame to symbolize how the Church was born. But it is not difficult to find examples of changed lives, or heroic men and women who, in the power of the Spirit, have dedicated themselves to works of teaching and healing and caring in dangerous and disease-ridden parts of the world. Have you not heard what Mother Teresa has done for the street castaways of Calcutta, or what Father Bruce Ritter has done for the street castaways of New York? And of course all around us there are less spectacular instances of men and women who have been possessed by a power which transforms selfishness, lust, and greed into unselfishness, love, and generosity.

When we compared the ant's-eye view of its world with the man's-eye view of it, we noted the difference between a narrow, limited view and a much bigger, more comprehensive view. We were concerned with the great contrast between the on-the-spot view of a moving, working multitude and a panoramic view of it from above. But there is another crucial distinction between an on-the-spot view and a supernatural view. It is the distinction between an outside view and an inside view.

I suppose we now have microscopes so fine, X-ray systems so sharp, and photographic machinery so refined that we can get an inside view even of so small a creature as the ant. Certainly we can get revealing inside pictures of the human body. No one, however, pretends that this kind of inside-view casts light on the working of the human mind and the human will. And therefore we cannot produce pictorial evidence of whatever it is within the human being that motivates his actions and determines his feelings and responses. Yet the one thing that is clear about the Holy Spirit is that he works within us. How then can we see him at work? If a court were to require evidence that a convicted man were cruel, the prosecuting counsel would have to point to a bruised child or a battered wife. It would be no good trying to focus on something within the man. The only valid evidence of a man's cruelty would be his external acts.

The Holy Spirit works within men and women. For others the only valid evidence of his power will be their external acts. So the difficulty of thinking about the Holy Spirit is not exactly the same as the difficulty of thinking about God the Creator or God the Son. When God made the world, when God sent his Son to redeem us, these were not events inside you and me. But when God the Holy Spirit acts, that is very definitely inside you and me and our like. The Holy Spirit is that spark of the divine within us which impels towards good and not towards evil.

You will read theologians who will say that the Church has been neglectful of the Holy Spirit in its teaching or in its worship. That is like complaining that a public speaker has said too little about his voice. There is no need for him to talk about his voice. His voice does the talking. Every word he utters is his voice in action. And every true sermon preached, every sound Sunday school lesson given, every prayer said, every hymn or psalm sung, is the Holy Spirit in action. And the Holy Spirit does not go to sleep between Sundays or even between services. Every impulse of your heart or mine that is not infected by selfishness or sin, but is directed towards the glory of God or the service of others is the impulse of the Holy Spirit.

The exciting thing about the Christian life is that day after day, hour by hour, minute by minute, we are being used by God in the power of the Holy Spirit—or we are refusing to be so used. And if the everywhere-present, always-pressing struggle between good and evil which this implies does not strike you as a valid presentation of the life we live today, then you and I are not meeting as minds.

There used to be a popular phrase about "jumping on the bandwagon." It described how quick-witted people with an eye on the main chance, seeing a vehicle rolling forward on the road to success and popularity, might seize the opportune moment and leap on it before it sped on to leave them behind forever. Well, the bandwagon makes a big noise and you jump on it if you want to be "in" with the popular trend of the moment. But there is a sense in which the Holy Spirit drives a bandwagon through history. It is not heading for immediate worldly success or prosperity. But it is leading all forces of good on this planet of ours. It is the only procession that is heading for heaven. Its call will stir us in our own hearts if we pause to listen to it. And if we don't mind the risk of leaving the comforts of our familiar ways behind us, it might be a good idea to take a running jump.

No sooner has one conjured up an image of this kind than one wants to throw it away. After all, as a hundred hymns tell us, the Holy Spirit works quietly with the secret hearts of men and women. There is no blare of public triumph surrounding the work of the Spirit. Even so, notions of the comforting, gentle, inner touch of the Spirit, which brings peace and assurance, need to be balanced by notions of power so violent that it can throw formerly timid men and women into the mouths of lions. The first manifestation of the Holy Spirit was like a whirlwind. And the gabble of the scene that followed seems to have resembled a multi-lingual Stock Exchange at a moment when indices are shooting up and down like rockets and thunderbolts. When T.S. Eliot wanted a forceful new image of the way the Holy Spirit descends upon the Church he compared it with the descent of a dive-bomber in an incendiary raid, breaking the air with tongues of flame. The "one discharge from sin and error" is an explosive and consuming fire.

The Holy Spirit is within us, directing our consciences, prompting us to acts of unselfishness, impelling us to pray. But he is not primarily a soothing, sustaining comforter. He is more like a dynamo than a soporific.

THIRTEEN

Unity in the Spirit

WHEN YOU ARE A LITTLE CHILD, a sore throat is one thing, an earache is another thing, a running nose is a third thing, and a headache is a fourth thing. And you feel especially aggrieved if two or three of these separate miseries strike you together. But when you are an adult you recognize them as all part of a single complaint, a chill, or perhaps influenza, and you are surprised if you get one of these symptoms without getting two or three others at the same time. Growing to understanding of things is often a matter of learning what connections there are beween them. When a student first begins to learn Latin and French they are totally different studies for him. But as he advances in knowledge of the two languages he comes to see the connections between them: the one is a later, modified version of the other.

People complain a lot these days about the way men and women have to work in separate compartments, one specializing in this and another in that. One works in computers and another in market gardening, and there does not seem to be much connection between the two. It may be difficult to launch a conversation that takes in the interests of both.

Human experience in general is divided up into departments in our minds. If we picture a nation at work, for instance, we think of all the people who grow living things on the land, producing crops or cattle, in one category. In another category we think of those who produce and process raw materials like coal, oil, steel, or rubber. Then there are those who manufacture finished products like clothing or cars or radios. Next come those who provide what are called "services"—basic and essential services like power, transport, the water supply, and so on; welfare services like education, hospitals, provision for the disabled, and social guidance; and leisure services like sport, drama, literature, television, tourism, and the like. On top of all this is the administrative layer that organizes our public affairs, makes sure that it works, and writes it all down on paper; and the governmental layer which in the long run controls the whole setup.

Our picture of a community is a picture of diverse activities meshing together—or sometimes failing to mesh. It is true that people who belong to different groupings may be pulled together by shared aims. Those who vote Republican or Conservative are linked together across the old boundaries of profession or class. Yet they are linked together across the old boundaries only by the erection of a "new" boundary which cuts them off from those who vote Democratic or Labor.

Religion is, or ought to be, a unifying influence. If people worship a common Father who made them and a common Savior who redeemed them, they are certainly pulled together into a new relationship. It is an external relationship based on common attachment to what is outside themselves—their Father in heaven and their Savior at his side. But as soon as you take the Holy Spirit into your calculations you are dealing with a power *inside* yourselves, inside you and me, him and her, pulling us all together, not by a common aim or a common attachment to something or someone outside ourselves, but by a living kinship in our souls.

We have distinguished the man's-eye view from the God's-eye view, the small limited view from the big timeless view, the view of the outside only from the view of the inside too. We have to move a step further in this argument which has shown the God's-eye view to be bigger and more penetrating than the man's-eye view. By penetrating within us the God's-eye view sees the same Holy Spirit operative in each one of us. This activity of the Holy Spirit pulls together the human beings it affects into a bonded relationship. So the God's-eye view, which the Christian will in his small way enter upon, is not only a bigger view and a more penetrating view, it is also a more unified view. The vast human family of Christian men and women are seen as indwelt by a single divine Spirit.

The unifying view is not, however, limited to our thinking about the human race. For the Holy Spirit is active in showing forth God's glory in the world he has made. Poets in all ages have expressed their sense of awe before the beauty of the natural world and many have tried, like Wordsworth for instance, to define their response to natural beauty in a way which reckons with the sensed living power of the God who made and sustains it. Wordsworth speaks of the power which dwells in sunsets, seas, the air,

And the blue sky, and in the mind of man;
A motion and a spirit, that impels
All thinking things, all objects of all thought,
And rolls through all things.

Now Wordsworth was not writing a sermon or a theological treatise when he wrote these lines. He was writing a poem in which he struggled to define, as honestly and vividly as he could, what his own living experience was and what it meant. That experience was like making contact with an indwelling spirit that moves the whole natural world and the minds of thinking men alike.

Perhaps the Christian is now, today, in the twentieth-century West, the only kind of person who thinks naturally and unforcedly of a united world, a world of all inanimate and living things bound together; because the Christian alone has this sense of the indwelling Spirit which the Father and the Son let loose on the universe and on mankind. Who, apart from the Christian, can shift his glance from the tree growing in his garden or the comet flashing across the sky to the baby in its pram without mentally jumping over barriers that separate one kind of experience from another? For the Christian, the physical world and the human family are one unified creation, and the evidence of that unity impinges on his consciousness in millions of ways. When he is moved by the beauty of a purple sunset on the hills, he senses the touch of the Creator. When he is moved by the sight of his gurgling baby in his cot, he senses the touch of the Creator. When he is moved by loving eyes or kind eyes, by joy shared or grief shared, he senses the touch of the Creator. When he encounters the seemingly inexplicable evocative power of a piece of music, a poem, or a painting, he senses the touch of the Creator. The Spirit within him and within others, and the Spirit evidenced in the natural world and the creations of men's hands and minds, is one and the same Spirit.

One of the Christian's most difficult tasks is to convey to non-Christians his sense of the unity of creation. Contemporary skepticism is heavily reliant on the distribution of blinkers to the population at large. The blinkers ensure that those who wear them will only see one thing at once, and that in total isolation from its larger context. If you look coldly at the world of trees and stones, cows and jellyfish, it has a kind of crude mindlessness that seems far away from the mental world where poets rhapsodize and philosophers philosophize. If you look coldly at the world of space enveloping our universe, the whole massive fabric has a kind of chill heartlessness that seems remote from what happens when a human couple fall in love or when a grandmother breathes her last. Over against the vast cosmic and natural machinery investigated by astronomers, geologists, zoologists, botanists, and a dozen other specialists, the world where a saint claims to have seen a vision or a mystic claims to have communed with Almighty God seems, not just fanciful, not just eccentric, but something apart, something separate.

The Christian's view is a unifying view which has no difficulty in seeing these things as all part of a common pattern. The Christian's difficulty, indeed, is to enter into the anti-Christian mind which separates them in such a way that they appear to be antithetical or even irreconcilable. The indwelling Spirit thus determines the Christian's outlook on all things. The

Christian is not in an alien world except insofar as other people make it so by denying the unity sensed by the Christian in the whole order of being, animate and inanimate. It is the Holy Spirit that makes you feel at home in God's world and homeless in man's rival world. It is the Holy Spirit that makes you feel angry with those who see nothing around them but machinery, conflict, and chaotic randomness.

FOURTEEN

Grace

A T THIS POINT I CAN IMAGINE that a critical reader might protest, "Wait a minute. I understand what you mean by saying that there is this divine Spirit at work in the natural world and in men and women. But if that is the case why do Christians pray for the Holy Spirit to descend upon them? Why do they sing hymns like, "Come, thou Holy Spirit, come!"? Surely this is unnecessary. If the Spirit is everywhere and in all things you can't help having your little bit of him, can you?"

"Little bit" is perhaps a useful expression in this argument. It would be fair to say that all men and women have something called "vitality." If they hadn't, they would be dead. But that does not prevent an athlete from training rigorously to conserve and increase his vitality or an overweight man from restricting his eating to increase his vitality. And when you say of someone that he has "little vitality" you are not drawing attention to his spark of life but to his near moribundity. I do not know whether any living human being is ever totally devoid of the least breath of the Spirit. I suspect that the doctrine that God has created and sustains the universe and its inhabitants means precisely that nothing can subsist if the heartbeat of the Spirit within it has finally failed.

We have got to use our God-given reason to examine what the doctrine of the Spirit logically amounts to. We who believe that God created all things and that his providence watches over all things assume that when a Christian manages to treat generously someone who has grievously damaged him, that is the work of God in him. Can we at the same time believe that when a virtuous unbeliever dives into the sea, saves someone from drowning, and loses his own life, the act is one from which the hand of God has been totally absent? No human being who believes in God the Creator can deny his part in whatever good there is in the world around us and in the hearts and wills of our fellow creatures.

We cannot separate the three persons of the Trinity, Father, Son, and Holy Spirit. We know from Christ's own words that he and the Father "are one." The Bible tells us how Jesus taught his apostles during his earthly life "through the Holy Spirit" and made his power permanently available to them after his ascension in the Holy Spirit. When we speak of a person taking Christ into his life, making Christ his permanent guide and companion, we are referring to the same process as when we speak of a person being possessed by the Holy Spirit. So there need be no embarrassment for us in switching from the one expression to the other. Where the Son is there the Father is also. Where the Spirit is there the Son is also. From the first the Bible describes the apostles as "full of the Holy Spirit."

Thus when we speak of the Holy Spirit impelling us to pray to Christ for help we are speaking quite logically and rationally, but we are not referring to two persons separate from each other in the way that you and I are separate. We are distinguishing usefully between the inner impulse and the outer personal appeal. In his illuminating book, *Saving Belief,* Austin Farrer has compared personal conversion to the capture of a town. The town is taken "by the joint effort of an assault from without and a fifth column within. Apart from the pressure from without, the fifth column would be held down. Apart from the action of the column, the assault would not breach the defenses."

The image is a helpful one. It was used long ago in a poem by John Donne. Donne describes himself as a usurped town, a town sold out treacherously to the Devil because God's "viceroy" in it, the human reason, has proved too weak and disloyal to defend it. Donne calls upon God to besiege the town, to batter, blast, and burn its defences to smithereens. This is the measure of a deeply felt personal need for the cleansing and remaking which man of his own resources is powerless to achieve and which only God can effect.

We have arrived thus at the doctrine of Grace. Having established that all goodness is the work of God, we have naturally accepted that when a man does what is good and right, that is the work of the Spirit within him. Knowing man's native tendency to sin, we know that man is dependent upon God for every impulse to resist temptation. The more we advance in the Christian life the more desperate we recognize this dependence to be. It takes a deeply prayerful convert like John Donne to conceive of himself as a living town usurped by the Devil, and to feel the need to cry out to God to take him by storm at any cost in pain and humiliation, for that is what Donne's prayer amounts to.

Now a skeptical reader might well object that God has been somewhat unfair to mankind in allowing us to drift into a situation so desperate. But human beings differ from all other things in our known universe in being created in God's image. God is our maker and he has made us all little makers too. We have to cooperate in his activity of making—even in his activity of making ourselves. This is the source of all our privileges, the secret of our freedom, and the explanation of our dire need. We alone of living beings have to cooperate in making ourselves, in gaining for ourselves true existence.

Even certain common idioms show our awareness of this truth. G.K. Chesterton once observed that you might slap a man on the shoulder who was drinking too heavily and say, "Be a man!", but it would be pointless to tell a recalcitrant crocodile to "be a crocodile." It can't fail to be a crocodile. But we can fail to be men and women, fail to be human. For the human being is made in God's image to love and serve his Maker and his fellows. And if a thing fails of its essential purpose, it fails to exist. A fire which fails to burn is not a fire. A seat which collapses when you sit on it is for practical purposes no longer a seat.

That is why we need education while animals do not. A lamb

will skip about on its legs soon after it is born. A human baby needs two or more years and a good deal of patient tuition to get to that stage. We have heard how a child brought up in India among wolves walked naturally on all fours. It is within the choice of any of us to walk or not to walk. A lamb separated from its mother and its flock and brought up as a domestic pet might make a very nice tame companion, but it would not begin to walk on two legs, even if you tried to teach it. Nor would it forget its bleating and learn to speak. Men and women can virtually turn into animals, but even faithful and friendly dogs and horses stop well short of turning into human beings. The better they are as dogs and horses, the more we like them.

And the more human human beings are, the more we approve of them. Education is, or ought to be, the process that turns us into fully human beings. Which means that it will try to turn us into the beings God made us to be.

It is a grave thing to say, but "secular education" is a contradiction in terms. True education would try to mold us in the image of Christ. It would insist that no progress in any sphere of knowledge or activity can be a substitute for learning to know, to love, and to serve God. And such knowledge, such love, and such service are the gifts of grace. "By Grace ye are saved," St. Paul said. By grace alone can we become human.

That is why civilization is now in danger of returning to the jungle.

FIFTEEN

The Incarnation

GRACE IS GOD IN ACTION IN US. The Holy Spirit is God in action in us and in our world. Providence is God in action in history. Jesus Christ was God in action in history. The Church is God in action in history. The critic might well say, "You Christians seem to be able to describe anything you approve of as 'God in action.'" To which we reply, "Exactly. You have hit the nail on the head." For indeed we Christians, if we are genuine, if we are sincere, cannot think or talk seriously about anything without coming back to God. There he is, making, sustaining, loving, saving us—and doing it in so many ways that, as we respond to them, we have to roll out different words: Creator, Redeemer, Sanctifier; Providence, Salvation, Grace.

God made us so many miniature "gods," so many creatures with, like himself, the ability to will and to make. Miniature "gods" share another distinction too. They can separate their thinking from what they are and where they are. The cow in the field outside looks contented. I can stare through the window at it and say, "For all its contentment, thank God I'm not a cow, especially on a cold, wet morning like this." But the cow cannot stare back through the window at me and say, "Thank God I'm not a human being, penned in a box like that with nothing to eat." Still less can it say, "I wish I could exchange with that fellow, sit in a warm room, walk about on my back legs, pick up food with my front legs, and give my neck a rest."

Not only can we think ourselves into the skins of cruder, more

73

limited beings like cows, we can also think ourselves into the individualities of higher or less limited beings. Our writers invent creatures like Ariel, Peter Pan, and Gandalf, as well as Caliban and Gollum. We can imagine ourselves able to fly. We can imagine ourselves as disembodied beings able to move through walls and have the advantages of invisibility.

Moreover we can talk about the man's-eye view—which is the only view we have—as though it were not the only view. I spoke about a God's-eye view, the view of a being able to look down on history, uplifted above time and space, and everyone knew at once what I meant. What an astonishing capacity this is. Strictly speaking, no man has ever experienced anything except the man's-eye view of his world. Yet one can talk of that view as something which one can temporarily escape from, temporarily rise above. This fact in itself is sure proof of man's creation by a God who intended him for something higher than his limited life in time.

Intended us; but did not compel us to cooperate. How could he compel us? We were miniature "gods" made in his own image, and no one compelled him.

Yet there could be no question of letting things be when, as a race, we opted for selfishness and sin. A God who makes, sustains, and loves the world and its inhabitants is not going to see it roll out of his control into destruction.

He sent his Son to save us. The divine became human. That is the doctrine of the Incarnation: that Jesus Christ was God in human flesh. This is obviously at one and the same time a simple thing to grasp and a profound thing to understand. And like all the simplest and profoundest matters in human experience, it is fatally easy to misunderstand and to misrepresent it.

Why do we need such an elaborate word as "Incarnation"? Cannot we just say, "God sent his Son"? We can, but we need to make sure that we are not misrepresenting what happened. God did not say to his Son, "Those people are in a mess down there. Go down and sort them out. Warn them what they are in for if they don't pull their socks up. Perform a few miracles to make sure there's no mistake about who you are. Then tell them where they stand. They don't deserve a second chance, but I'm going to give them one. After all, what Adam let them in for happened a long time ago. So don't be too rough on them. But leave them in no doubt that sin has got to stop!"

It might have been like that. But it wasn't. Christ's earthly life was not a kind of inspectorial visitation authorized by an offended but well-disposed overlord to administer a healthy rebuke, a warning, and an order to do better in the future.

Nor did God say, "Look here, these people down there have gone badly astray, but I'm still fond of them, I'm afraid. It's no good playing the heavy Father and sending someone to tell them where they get off. It would only make them more resentful. You've got to get in touch with people where they are. You've got to get down to their own level. You've got to make them feel, 'He's a good sort. He's one of us really. He doesn't put on airs.' Then they'll take some notice of you and you'll get a genuine response. So I think you'd better go down there disguised as a man. There needn't be anything deceitful about it. Without making too much fuss you can come clean with them about who you are if they press you or if the situation seems to demand it. But be right in among them, because they're not going to take straight instructions from anyone. Time was when I could issue Ten Commandments just like that, and the best of them would fall in immediately. But that old authoritarianism is finished. You've got to treat people like equals and persuade them to participate with you. So gather a little group around you to help, and don't hesitate to mix with a few down-and-outs. Then people will learn from you at first hand what being a real person means, and they might even become a bit ashamed and apologetic for having been so difficult."

It might have been like that. But we can be sure it was not. God did not dress up as a man just in order to provide a vivid corrective example of what being a human being ought to mean. Christ's human life was not primarily a cunningly devised divine exercise in mucking in, being one of the boys, and so winning a sympathetic ear from grateful acquaintances.

We are not going to be so presumptuous as to try to imagine what words might exactly express God's intention in the Incarnation. But we know that Christ was not sent just to instruct or set an example. He was not sent only like a prophetic teacher or even a specimen saint. He was sent to be a human being, to be fully so from cradle to grave. Not to play a part on a stage from which he could, if necessary, run back to the dressing-room at any moment and get back into his own clothes. He was sent to suffer and to die. And insofar as there was a living example here, it had a double validity. For the example did not only indicate: "This is what being a human being means," it also indicated: "This is what being God means."

Perhaps one should amend the latter sentence to, "This is part of what being God means," because of course being God also means looking down on time and mankind from eternity, holding the world in his hand. It means what the Father does as well as what the Son does, not to mention the Holy Spirit. It means loving protectively and it means loving self-sacrificially. It means authority and creation: it means obedience and self-abnegation. The divine family in heaven is a family of equal persons, Father, Son, and Holy Spirit, just as the human family on earth is a family of equal persons, man, wife, and the offspring of both. Yet authority and obedience and what proceeds from them are properly at work in both families.

A God who knows exactly what it is to eat a meal and take a walk, to have toothache or stomachache, to rejoice at a wedding or to mourn at a funeral, to be indebted to an earthly mother and her husband, to stand trial in a human court, to be flogged, to be cruelly executed, does not need to apologize to men and women for his immunity, still less for his existence.

SIXTEEN

Evil

MUCH HAS BEEN SAID in this book about God's activity in making and sustaining our world and ourselves. God has been described as the source of all things. The first question that leaps to the mind of every thoughtful man or woman is "Why does he allow evil?" We may be said to have answered that question in showing how man's freedom to be himself a maker and a chooser left the way open for him to err. But that does not get to the root of the matter for most people. They might well protest, "You have explained how God allowed men to choose evil. But why was evil there to be chosen? You say God made everything. Why did he make evil?"

The answer is that evil was never "made." Evil does not have the kind of substantial existence that good has. This does not mean that evil is an "unreal" in the sense of "imaginary" thing that is projected into the universe by the human mind. It means that, although it is not wrong to picture man standing at a junction with a signpost that points to "Good" in one direction and to "Evil" in another, it is absolutely wrong to imagine that the "Evil" road leads anywhere at all. The "Good" sign points, we may say, to a solidly constructed city with a highway leading to it. The "Evil" sign is deceptive in that it points only to a morass; for the road peters out. It only *looks* like a valid alternative. Indeed, if we did not allow ourselves to be deceived, we should recognize that there is only one road. If you leave it, you wander off into the desert.

God made the city and God made the road. The appearance

of an alternative road is an illusion. You can stay on the road and get somewhere, or you can leave it and get lost. That is the choice life offers.

There is no evil that is not goodness corrupted, or goodness perverted. We can perhaps understand this most easily in relation to material things. We said that a chair which collapses when you sit on it is for practical purposes not a chair at all. We call it a "bad" chair, a "defective" chair, a "broken" chair, but there is no evading the fact that the worse it is, the less it is effectively a chair—i.e., something you can sit on. So all talk about its being a "bad" or "worse" or "defective" chair is simply talk about its not being a chair at all.

Now "chair-ness" is plainly a good thing. It's nice and useful to have something to sit on. But the "badness," the "defective-ness," the "broken-ness" of a chair is *nothing at all*: it is a way of describing the material's *failure* to be a chair. There is "chair-ness" and there is "lack of chair-ness," and you can make your choice between them. When we say that a carpenter has made a "bad" chair, because a leg has broken when someone tried to sit on it, we clearly mean that he has failed to make a true chair. It is not making, but failure of making, that produces defects.

"When I looked inside the room I saw that they had stripped him naked and lain him on a metal stand, more like an ironing-board than a bed. A harsh light shone down just above his body. There were four masked figures bending silently over him. They looked like members of the Ku Klux Klan. One was holding a cap over the victim's face. It appeared that some chemical was being used to immobilize him. I saw one of the masked men take a gleaming knife and thrust it into his side."

Is this the description of a torture-chamber or of an operating theater? Clearly it might be either. The one is an evil thing, the other a good thing. What essentially distinguishes the one from the other is the different human motives behind what is happening.

An interesting thing is that when evil men want to torture to the utmost, they become conscious of this peculiar superficial relationship between evil and good. Fiction writers often exploit this fact. The Secret Police at their most vicious and cruel use the vocabulary of goodness and kindness for their torture. The sinister agents of evil, determined to get their victim to talk, fall back on fake friendliness, fake sincerity, and fake kindness. "Come now, a little hospital treatment would do you a world of good. We'll have you in the . . . er . . . operating theater in a jiffy . . . and you'll come out a new man, with a totally different outlook. You've no idea how well-disposed you'll feel to us when our . . . er . . . surgeons and anaesthetists have put you through their latest . . . remedial treatment. I think you'll come round beautifully afterwards . . . I hope so. The treatment is a novel one: it uses all the refinements of modern medical know-how. And we've had a hundred percent success rate with it so far. Everyone who has been through it has proved grateful afterwards. They've become really trustful, reliable friends, keeping no secrets from us at all."

When you come up against the worst kind of evil, you recognize that it is essentially *parodic*. It is a mock-up travesty of goodness. The worst kind of hostility turns out to be fake friendliness, the worst kind of falsehood is fake sincerity, the worst kind of cruelty is fake kindness. All evil desire parodies good desire. Thieves desire for themselves things that are good in themselves, beautiful possessions; gluttons desire things that are good in themselves, steaks and strawberries; debauchees desire things that are in themselves good, the bodies of beautiful women; even corrupt tyrants often desire what is good in itself, an orderly harmonious society living in prosperity and peace.

The more you search for evil as something in itself substantial, the more elusive it seems. That is not to question the "reality" of evil. Evil is real enough—but only by derivation, by parasitism, by parody. When the little boy kicks the kitten, the action is not physically different from kicking a football. The leg is a good leg, the movement a good movement, the impulse to exercise himself is healthy. Evil can be located only in exploiting those good resources and impulses to an unworthy end. It is not kicking that is evil, but the perversion of a healthy act to a cruel purpose.

One great writer who understood the nature of evil perfectly was John Milton. He was so sensitive to the parasitical and parodic nature of evil that in *Paradise Lost* he projected his Satan as a mock-up divinity. There is nothing done by Satan in Milton's *Paradise Lost* that does not in some way parody God's thought and his work. Satan is a mock-up divinity destroying man in parodic imitation of God's work in creating and saving man. So successful was Milton in presenting Satan as a mock-up divinity mouthing the vocabulary of goodness that, as Christian influence decayed, readers and critics began to say, "Satan is really Milton's hero." What they meant (had they understood what they meant) was that, seeing the real God and the mock-up God (who is the Devil) confronting each other, they recognized that their own God was the mock-up one. Milton's psychological masterstroke in showing human beings where they really stand has been in that respect the most astonishing literary achievement of Christendom.

Suppose you missed the irony and the parody in our Secret Policeman's talk to his victim, would you not say, "Here is a kindhearted, well-meaning official indeed"?

In life, as in literature, it is very easy to mistake the fake for the genuine. Even Christianity can be turned into a parody of itself. (It is happening all around us.)

If people ask, "Why did God make evil?" the proper reply is that everything God made is good. Only *unmaking* can produce evil. If the further question is asked, "Why had goodness to be of such a kind that it could be parodied by evil?" the only reply is that it is a mystery. That is the kind of world we live in. Just as ours is a world where three-legged men with eyes in their shoulder-blades are inconceivable, so a world where goodness is unpervertable is inconceivable.

The Christian must always be ready to accept that there are unfathomable mysteries. There are bound to be where there is an unfathomably omnipotent and mysterious God. St. Augustine tells of a questioner who asked, "What was God about before he made the world?" and was answered, "He was making hell for those who pry into his mysteries."

SEVENTEEN

God in Action

IT IS NOT DIFFICULT TO PROVE that we live in a wicked world. And it is not difficult to accept that the world was made by a good God. The difficulty arises when people begin to query the connection between these two facts. The peculiarity of Christianity is that it sees human history, not just as a long struggle between good people and bad people, but also as a long struggle between God and human selfishness.

The word "struggle" is used purposefully. Without some such word we cannot make sense of the central event in history, the crucifixion of Christ.

It is tempting to picture God in heaven, looking down on the world he has made, and "tut-tutting" over the mess that men and women have got themselves into. "Dear Me! Whatever will they do next?" For it is natural to assume that human wickedness distresses God. After all he made men and women in his own image and gave them a beautiful world to dwell in. They have scarcely rewarded his generosity with the obedience and love which it ought to have called out. What is difficult for many people to conceive is that God has been campaigning through history to get the better of human disobedience. "Campaigning" is perhaps not the best word because it suggests a lot of talking and preaching, stumping the countries of the world and trying to drum up support for the party that will put things right. God's campaign on earth did not culminate in his being publicly swept to power. It was a long struggle, conducted through the lives and teaching of the

81

patriarchs and prophets to prepare the way for his personal intervention. And its climax was Christ's death on the cross.

To be fair, the pollsters never gave the campaign much prospect of success. There was never a stage at which the popular ratings showed a majority, or even a substantial percentage, of the human race in favor of a return to obedience to God. Yet God did not fail. He did not lose the long struggle. The crucifixion was followed by the resurrection.

When we read the Old Testament and the New Testament we find that we are faced by a long record of encounters between God and his people. When we lay the Bible aside and return to our daily preoccupations, it is fatally easy to lose entirely this awareness of continuing confrontation between God and the human race. It is not that we cease to believe in God as the Bible is closed in our hand or the church door is closed behind us, but I suspect that we begin to believe in a rather different kind of God. He may have been very evidently active down here when Noah set about building the ark under his instructions or when the Red Sea opened to let the escaping Israelites through, but we don't look for that kind of divine intervention today. Again he may have been very evidently active down here when our Lord gave the dumb man speech and raised Lazarus from the dead, but obviously the Son of God is not threading his way through our streets in the flesh today.

So we fall back, naturally, on a picture of human life which God surveys from a distance. Yes, we assume that there are things he strongly approves of, like evangelistic campaigns or Mother Teresa's heroic efforts for the poor and sick in Calcutta. And we know there are things he strongly disapproves of, like murders and rapes in our cities and cruelly unjust imprisonments in Russia or Poland. But we don't think of God being involved in it all in the degree to which he was involved when he gave marching orders to Abraham or blinded Saint Paul on the road to Damascus.

We find it easier to think of an approving God and a disapproving God than an active God. Indeed for the most part we tend to conceive of God, not as a participator in human history, but as a spectator of human history. We picture human history as being enacted on a kind of stage in the theater of the universe. Those who performed in earlier acts and have left the earthly scene sit down there in the Stalls as present-day history passes before their eyes. Meanwhile the angels—or whatever supernatural beings there are—look down on the stage from the Dress Circle. God, of course, sits in the Royal Box, the Son at his side, and the Holy Spirit hovering nebulously in the background. There is plenty in the performance that he finds regrettable; but when he founded the theater he decided to abolish censorship, so for the most part he puts up with it. Just occasionally he tells the Holy Ghost to inform the management that it's time a certain actor left the company. And once or twice he has been known, after witnessing a superbly fine performance, to send for the actor or actress, give them a special commendation, and call for three cheers for them from the Stalls and the Circle.

I am trying to parody our fatal notion of the gap between active human history and an observant God, a watching supervisor. God is not an observer. Insofar as there is a human drama he is the central figure in it, even if his role often seems like that of the Invisible Man.

We have got into the way of mentally tearing God out of the world he has made and which he daily sustains. We have opted for an absent God, and then we complain because we see no sign of his presence. And when he has plainly acted, as in the manner recorded in the Bible, we have tended to turn the action into a kind of object lesson; we have tended to say, "Ah yes, this event shows that he is a God of love; this event shows that he is a God of forgiveness; this event shows that he is a God of joy." All very true, but all gross understatements. What God has done in history has not been simply to give a series of practical lessons to instruct us. For just as God is not a member of the audience watching human history, so too he is not a teacher standing in front of his human children and giving them instructive lessons. He did not call upon Abraham to sacrifice Isaac merely to provide humanity with an object lesson in faith. And he did not send his only-begotten Son to the cross simply to provide humanity with an object lesson in love.

We have all got into the habit of conducting our religious thought and discussion on the "This shows that" principle. This shows that God is kind, or merciful, or long-suffering. As though God said to himself, "Now today I must arrange an incident that will show these men and women how just I am or how loving I am." Christian teaching is in danger of being turned into a collection of specimens illustrative of virtue as opposed to vice. God is in danger of being turned into a schoolmaster. The only safeguard against this kind of attitude is to realize that the whole Christian story is the record of God's acts.

The climax of these acts, the crucifixion of God himself, is the most revealing of all he did. When a man dives into the sea to save a drowning child and risks his life in the act, you can safely guess what is in his mind. It is primarily, "I must save that child, whatever the risk." It is not primarily, "I must provide an example of self-sacrifice to show others how to live." At the moment of decision the man is determined to do his best to save the child. If he fails to save the child he fails, whether he himself survives or drowns. If he saves the child he succeeds, whether he himself survives or drowns.

The Son of God came to earth to save mankind whatever the personal cost. Human sinfulness crucified him. There was a straight struggle between God and man's corrupted will. But if God in Christ did indeed save mankind, then he succeeded in his purpose.

EIGHTEEN

The Crucifixion

THE CHRISTIAN REVELATION is a record of what God has done (and is doing). It is therefore a kind of history. And history differs from some other subjects of study (such as philosophy, for instance) in that it presents you first and foremost with hard facts. A historian can of course build theories around the facts. He can interpret what happened by saying, "This or that war was obviously the consequence of economic greed on the part of both contestants." But he cannot adjust the facts to the theories. The Christian theologian is in this respect in the same position as the historian. He has the facts before him, recorded in the Old and New Testaments. On these he bases his theories of God and his dealings with men.

There are some branches of study which are not quite so firmly tied to external facts as history is and theology is, or should be. For instance, the philosopher may build a theory on notions that are the fruit of inner reflection rather than of external observation. "I think, therefore I am," Descartes asserted. Similarly, psychologists sometimes reason about the workings of the human mind in a way that wanders a long way from exactly observed human behavior.

Theology can never ignore or explain away the acts of God. And since it can never get the God's-eye view, it has to recognize the limitations of the man's-eye view. What it must never do is to pretend that the man's-eye view is final and absolute. Thus it can never say, "The man's-eye view cannot make sense of this, so it cannot have happened." If Jesus turned water into wine at a wedding or walked on the surface of the sea, then this is certainly evidence of his power over nature. What the Christian observer cannot do is to say, "Hold on. These are miracles. Such things do not happen." The evidence of history is that such things did happen.

They present us with a mystery. But what did we expect when we began to inquire into the source of all being in the universe, into the reality of the mind that conceived the Rocky Mountains and designed the brains that design computers? You cannot eliminate mystery from the world God made. How can you expect to eliminate mystery from the ways of its Maker?

The Crucifixion is on one level the most obvious event of Christian history and on another level the most mysterious fact of divine revelation. But then *all* human deaths are both obvious, in that they are natural and to be expected at some time or other, and mysterious in that they represent an apparently total denial of all that the living world of growth and beauty calls out in the human heart. If your death and mine is a matter of inexplicable awe and mystery, we can hardly expect God's to be less so.

Christ's death, we are told, involved the death of the old sinning Adam; his resurrection involved the birth of the new, redeemed, and re-created Adam. The two crucial truths that emerged were that sin was forgiven and new life gained. And if there is anything that natural human experience through the ages has hammered into men's hearts and minds, it is that wickedness is costly and birth is costly. Let us remember the facts and forget the theories for a moment. You cannot open a newspaper any day of the year without learning how costly in human suffering wickedness is. We learn it from a sensational murder trial; we learn it from accounts of privation and death in poor and war-torn corners of the earth. That birth is costly too every mother is aware.

God came to a world where birth is costly. He came to a world where vegetable and human life alike is renewed only through the cycle of death and burial. Was he likely to set all that aside in opening up his new creation? Did he come to turn the divinely created order upside down? God came to a world where human wickedness costs mountains of pain and rivers of blood. Was he likely to bypass that tremendous and terrible reality in lifting the burden of guilt from the human race? Are those who protest that the Crucifixion was unnecessary wanting a God who magics evil and death away with a conjuror's deftness and an illusionist's grin?

The suffering and death of Christ confirm all that we know of what evil extorts and what birth exacts. The Crucifixion calls us not to argument, but to reflection and prayer.

Not that logic and reason can be of no help to us in meditating on the Crucifixion. Robert Browning wrote a fine poem, *Saul*, which can aid us in trying to understand why Christ's death on the cross was inevitable. The poem tells, in David's own words, how he is called to King Saul's tent because it is hoped that he may be able to help the king, who dearly loves him and his harping. For Saul is lost to his surroundings in a trance of black depression. For three days he has been blind and dumb. In his agony Saul stands, erect and static, against the tent-prop, his arms stretched out along the cross-support. (It is as though he is crucified.) David sings to him songs of the country, of harvest, of marriage, of battle, of worship, and at last evokes a shudder from the tragic figure of Saul, the first sign of life. Then David sings of all the joys of life, of nature, human kinship, beauty, strength, love, and sovereignty; and at last Saul relaxes into awareness. But still the journey back to vitality and cheerfulness is only half traversed. So, wracking his brains, David sings in praise of the immortality of Saul's fame, and now the trance is broken. Saul wipes the sweat from his face, sinks to the ground, lays his hand on David's head, and surveys the youngster's face. But nothing is said. Saul may have been restored to movement, but he is still far from his vigorous, joyous self.

What can David do now? What more can he offer than earthly delight and immortal fame to make his king feel that life is worth living? In anguish he yearns, at any cost to himself, to be able to offer Saul some more overwhelming blessing still.

This anguish itself inspires David with a sudden new insight. He knows that in everything God surpasses man immeasurably—in wisdom and foresight, in the creation of magnificence and beauty. Yet he, David, loves Saul so deeply that he would suffer for him to gain for him, if he could, new life, and indeed everlasting life. The logic of this realization is stunning. If a man can love his fellowman so that he longs for everlasting life for him, and would himself suffer and die for him to attain it, then man is better than God—unless God would do, will do, the same.

In self-sacrifice, in laying down his life for another's well-being, man surpasses God in goodness and love, the creature surpasses the Creator. That is the absurdity that stares David in the face. And he cannot accept that a God who excels man so vastly in every other respect will be inferior to man in this most testing matter of all. So David's singing culminates in a prophetic vision of the future Christ.

The logic of this conclusion is forceful. Greater love hath no man than this, that a man lay down his life for his friends. There have been men and women in all ages who have devoted themselves to others at great personal cost and have sacrificed their lives for others. If there were nothing on God's part fully to match this capacity for the ultimate in acts of love and suffering, then indeed man could justly be said to be in some respects and on some occasions better than God. The creature would have the edge on the Creator.

This train of thought seems to point to the logical necessity for the crucifixion. But it is not followed here as an argument to *prove* anything. Rather it is a reflection on the crucifixion; just one attempt to ponder its mystery and to relate it understandably to our own human experience. We recognize the powerful logic binding together the most heroic self-sacrifices of loving men and women with the great redemptive work of their Maker. When we speak of God's power and wonder and beauty, we have sunsets and symphonies to point to. When we speak of God's illimitable love, our minds turn to Christ on the cross. And there is something inside us which knows that nothing less would serve.

NINETEEN

The Resurrection

IN VERDI'S OPERA, *Simone Boccanegra*, the story of a fourteenth-century Doge of Venice, there is a moving scene in which Simone, now in middle life, encounters the girl Amelia who turns out to be his own daughter. She is the child of Maria Fiesco. Maria died soon after Amelia's birth, and the child was lost in infancy. As Simone first begins to suspect who she is, the music reflects his inner perturbation and excitement. When the truth is made known, it rises to a rapturous emotional outburst such as Verdi was master of.

Any member of an audience would be stirred by the lyrical power of the mutual recognition between father and daughter. But if there were a man in the audience who had lost his own daughter in childhood, he would be doubly moved. And if that same man had lost his young wife by early bereavement too, he would be triply moved. The reflection of our own sufferings and joys in those of others works powerfully on our emotions.

But suppose this same man in the audience happened to know and to recollect that Verdi lost his young wife after a few short years of married life and lost his infant daughter and son too. He would say to himself, "The creator of this scene has lived through all the sufferings that these characters are represented as having lived through. He has lived through all the suffering and loss that I have lived through. And now he presents a moment of rapturous recovery such as all who have been thus bereaved dream of."

The gospel narrative of Christ's sufferings is such that there is no degree of unmerited human pain we can endure of which we cannot say, "God has lived through this too." Just as there is no degree of human love and self-sacrifice by which man can get the edge on God, so there is no degree of human suffering by which man can get the edge on God.

When you come to think of it, what *more* could be expected of the God who created us? And—to press an even sharper question—what *less* could be expected of the God who created us?

And what about that rapturous rediscovery, that restoration of the lost one, alive and whole? In the opera the creator provided it for his creatures—just as Shakespeare did in *A Winter's Tale* where the king discovers alive his supposedly dead wife and daughter after long years of grief.

The reader may say, "This is all very well. In stories and plays with happy endings people supposed dead are discovered to be alive and lost people are found. But real life, unfortunately, is not like that."

But if we argue like this, are we not in danger of falling back into the old error of assuming that we human beings can beat God at his own game? That Shakespeare's mind can make a world where suffering is swallowed up in joy, but that God can only make a world where suffering is triumphant and death ends everything? Were Shakespeare and Verdi kinder-hearted than God?

This is not in fact a trivial or gimmicky argument, as it might seem at first sight. Its apparent simplicity is deceptive, for it conceals a deep truth.

Indeed we are now at grips with perhaps the most decisive issues which divide believers from unbelievers. For it is nonsense to pretend any longer that the main intellectual struggle of Christianity is with science. The notion that modern science is in conflict with an outmoded religion, Christianity, will not bear examination. There is no science which does not today include convinced Christians among its most eminent specialists. It is plain that whatever issue is crucial in determining whether a man can accept the gospel of the death and resurrection of Jesus Christ, it cannot logically be a question of scientific credibility—though the unbeliever can always imagine or pretend to himself that it is.

The main *intellectual* obstacle to Christian belief is of a different character. The word "intellectual" is important, for in fact the real obstacles to belief are rarely intellectual. They are generally moral. People want to go their own sweet way. More often than not the supposed "intellectual" obstacles to belief are mere excuses which give a kind of respectability to selfishness and worldliness.

Be that as it may, the argument brought most powerfully against the Christian faith has two forms. There is Thomas Hardy's claim that human affairs are too prone to accident, suffering, and disaster for the world to be under the control of a benevolent God. The same view was voiced by the novelist Somerset Maugham. He could not believe in a loving God, he said, because he had seen little children dying in the hospital diphtheria wards.

These attitudes deserve respect in that they spring from sensitivity to the sufferings of our fellow beings. They spring from what can only be called "indignation" at the sight of human lives so sadly afflicted or awry.

The other form of this argument is that the gospel of the resurrection and the gift of everlasting life is an escapist dream. It is "too good to be true." The two forms of the argument are obviously two sides of the same coin. "The world is too bad for the Christian gospel to be true." "The gospel is too good to be believed."

But if there is a God who made the world and all that is in it, he not only gave life to the child dying of diphtheria, he also gave life to Somerset Maugham whose heart swelled with sorrow and indignation at the sight. If God is the First Cause of the child now struggling for breath, he is the First Cause of the doctor who is brimming over with grief and outrage at the sight of innocent suffering. We cannot trace all diphtheria back to God and attribute all righteous pity to man. Righteous pity and diphtheria belong to the same created world. We may not understand why the world had to be like that, but at least we know that there is a particular brand of costly loving-kindness which only innocent suffering could call out.

We cannot attribute life's negatives to our Creator and life's positives to ourselves. It can be argued that, far from being too good to be true, the Christian gospel is too good to be false. We have spoken of the absurdity of the idea of man's beating God at his own game. If man has invented Christianity, knocked up out of his own head the massive system of belief that binds all human suffering and joy together, indeed binds all human experience together in the drama of divine creation, redemption, and salvation, then indeed there can be no question about it. We human beings have got God whacked. He cannot hold a candle to us. In competition with us he is a non-starter. For what is the whole cosmos but a crude piece of engineering, when compared to the Christian message that turns all grief to joy, that swallows up sin in forgiveness, that promises to any human being the one thing which in his heart of hearts he longs for most yearningly: the gift of life beyond time, the knowledge that death is not the end?

TWENTY

Forgiveness

THE TWO MESSAGES which the early disciples carried about the world were that in Christ death was conquered and sins could be forgiven. "God for Christ's sake hath forgiven you," St. Paul said. The great parable of forgiveness is the story of the prodigal son who wasted all that was given him, then returned home to his father's house to say, "Father, I have sinned against Heaven and before thee and am no more worthy to be called thy son." And it is notable that he regards his offense as, firstly, against Heaven, and, secondly, against his father. There is no sin that is not in the first place sin against God.

It is important to remember this. Sometimes preachers quite rightly stress that we must forgive everyone their offenses against us, just as God forgives our offenses against him. Indeed St. Paul spoke like that in the passage we have quoted above. "And be ye kind one to another, tender-hearted, forgiving one another, even as God for Christ's sake hath forgiven you." The Lord's Prayer puts it the other way around. There we pray for God's forgiveness insofar as we ourselves forgive others. In practice many of us may have limited scope for forgiving others. An awful lot of the offenses which others commit, and which affect us, are only *partly* offenses against ourselves. And of course though we can forgive all offenses against ourselves we are not in a position to forgive offenses against others. Only the offended can forgive those.

You may "forgive" your son for stealing a cassette from a

shop, but that does not wipe out his offense. His offense was against the shop-keeper, to whom he must apologize and return the stolen goods or otherwise make amends, if he is going to obtain the only valid human forgiveness for the offense.

There can be something misleading and dangerously presumptuous in ready talk about the need for Christians to be "forgiving." Christ died on the cross, not primarily and directly to turn you and me into forgiving creatures, but to turn you and me into forgiven creatures. True, we can be forgiven only insofar as we are also forgiving, but the scope we have for forgiving is limited, whereas the scope we have for being forgiven is virtually limitless.

Suppose I have a valuable picture and an acquaintance who is in financial difficulties steals it. Then he suddenly feels ashamed of what he has done, comes to see me, returns the picture, and asks to be forgiven. It is within my power to say, "Agreed. We will forget all about it. Everything shall be as it was before between us." But suppose he sells my picture, settles his debts with the money obtained, and then suddenly feels ashamed of what he has done. He comes to see me. He cannot give me back my picture. He offers to recompense me as soon as he can afford to and asks my forgiveness. The issue is more complicated in that the effect of the offense cannot be wholly wiped out. I may suspect that, having solved his financial problem, he is now worried about possible detection and thinks it safer to square me before my next interview with the police on the matter. I might question whether I have the right to say, "Agreed. We will forget all about it," without first requiring him to explain himself to the police. For the picture was valuable and detectives are daily spending the taxpayers' money in trying to solve the case. I myself certainly cannot clear the thief's guilt.

And suppose again that, having stolen the picture, my acquaintance has reason to believe he is suspect. So he destroys the picture by burning it. Then suddenly he feels ashamed of what he has done. He asks me to forgive him. My scope for forgiveness is more limited still. The initial theft was an offense against me. But the destruction of the picture was not only an offense against me but against the artist who painted it and indeed against all art lovers the world over.

This point could be pressed further. Suppose a vandal were to destroy one of the world's greatest artistic treasures. Suppose he managed to defeat all the protective devices of the Louvre and irreparably damaged the *Mona Lisa*. And then suppose he was filled with remorse. Where is the committee of artists and art-lovers, however high-powered, who would have the effrontery to say, "In the name of the human race—and that includes all the billions of future tourists who will ever visit the Louvre— we forgive you"?

We test all human theories by applying them to extreme cases. If someone claims, "This clothing will keep a man warm anywhere on earth," then we want to know how it will stand up to use at the North Pole or in an ascent of Mount Everest. When we hear that we must be ready to forgive all men and women, even our enemies, we wonder whether this requires us to think kindly of Adolf Hitler and the Nazis who ran Belsen and Auschwitz. When we hear that all offenses should be forgiven, we ponder the case of the multiple-murderer who has raped and butchered a dozen girls and now sits in jail.

We are told not to judge. It is plain that we are not in a position to judge. And it is plain that the mountainous accumulation of human wickedness is beyond the reach of purely human forgiveness. To contemplate it, however, ought never to produce the reaction, "All this sinfulness is too vast for me to tackle by going into the forgiving business, so I'd better think about something else." It ought rather to produce the reaction, "This is what comes of human disobedience to God's law. And I have my own part in that disobedience."

In short we shall get nowhere in the Christian life by concentrating on our role as potential forgivers. We are the potentially forgiven.

The Bible uses the word "redeem" of Christ's saving work. He came to restore human beings to acceptable sonship of the Father as the prodigal son was restored. The word "redeem" has an archaic ring. It is still used by insurance companies and it was once used widely by pawnbrokers. If you "redeemed" your pawned silver teapot, you got it back into your possession as good as it was when you parted with it. There is a commercial flavor about the word in these usages. But not so when we speak of a person's faults and then say, "Ah, but he has one redeeming feature: he would give a helping hand to anyone in need." Here the word has a moral flavor. We feel that the man's kindness to the needy cancels out any defects he may have.

Christ's redemptive work on the cross was undertaken to cancel out human sins. But you could not even redeem an old overcoat from the pawnshop without producing your ticket. And your claim on Christ's redemptive work can be pressed only by presenting the ticket of penitence.

It is well that the business of obtaining God's forgiveness is so simple. For, God knows, as we have already shown, the business of seeking and obtaining—or even granting—human forgiveness may often be so tangled as to baffle us. But one thing is clear. When we are confronted by offenses against ourselves or by any wickedness of others, and no forgiving or corrective response seems possible, then there is only one thing for us to do, and that is to ask God's forgiveness for our own sins, and to pray that he will touch others with the grace of penitence.

In the long run, whatever the offense, God alone can remove guilt.

TWENTY-ONE

Love of God

THE BIBLE TELLS US that we must love God with all our hearts and our neighbors as ourselves. What does love of God mean?

Perhaps no word in the English language is used more loosely or more variously than the word "love." Let us look at some straightforward usages first. We say, "Tom loves his mother," "Edward loves his wife," or "Jimmy Smith loves Maggie Brown." Do we mean something very different when we speak of our duty to love God? It would seem not. For presumably we must try to please God as Tom tries to please his mother. We must work for God just as Edward works hard to give his wife what she wants. And we must seize every opportunity to be with God, as Jimmy Smith sneaks off whenever he can to be with Maggie Brown.

But of course there are many other uses of the word "love." We say, "Joan loves discos," "Sally loves hamburgers," "Kevin loves his violin," "Joe loves his dogs," "Ben loves his yacht," "Sue loves Chanel No. 5," "Paul loves the sea," or "Mike loves railroad trains." Is there anything to be learned from these usages of what love of God means?

If we think carefully about each instance we shall discover that perhaps there is. Joan rejoices in surrendering to the sway of the dance as we ought to rejoice in surrendering ourselves to God's vitality and guidance. Sally delights in drawing nourishment from hamburgers as we ought to delight in drawing nourishment from God. Kevin cherishes his violin and practices daily to make himself more intimate with its amazing potential, and so we must work daily at making ourselves more intimate with God. Joe never forgets when it is time to attend to his dogs, and we have to be mindful of our daily attention to what God expects of us. Ben rushes off every weekend to check up on whether there is something he ought to be doing for his yacht, just as we must check up weekly on what we ought to be doing for God. Even Sally's exhilaration when she is bathed in the fragrance of her favorite perfume reminds us how we ought to respond to God's nearness. As for Paul's sensitivity to the grandeur of the sea, it is not unlike the way the Christian must meditate adoringly on God's splendor and majesty. Lastly, the way Mike devours books in the evenings on the history of the railroad reminds us of our daily duty to study the history of God's revelation among us contained in the Bible.

So we need not regret the variety of ways in which the word "love" is used. Indeed this variety of usage indicates how far-reaching is the claim that God is Love and how far-reaching is the demand that we must love God. We must not separate our love for anything on earth that is good and worthy from our love of God.

We are not, after all, talking about something abstract and highly spiritualized when we talk about love of God. If God's love for us has provided in his created world things as delectable as hamburgers and Chanel No. 5, we must not imagine that those things are unworthy to be loved in his name, or that he cannot be loved as they are loved—provided that it does not stop at that; provided that our love for God includes many other longings, delights, and duties too.

We must be wary, then, of describing love of God by negatives. We are not even entitled to say, "Of course, it's quite different from feeling the need for another drink" (I'd love a glass of beer!), because we have the word of the psalmist that it is not: "Like as the hart desireth the waterbrooks, so longeth my soul after thee, O God." Perhaps after all it is not utterly different either from having your eye caught by a beautiful girl (I say, I'd love to chat up that blonde!), for love of God takes in all earthly desire and thirst and *so much more.* Love of God takes it in cleansed of its selfishness, of its irresponsibility, of its urge to exploit.

We do not have to try to turn ourselves into disembodied beings in order to love God. He did not create the world with all its wonders, and ourselves with all our senses that delight in them, in order that we should turn our backs on his handiwork whenever we try to talk to him. If you were to have the privilege of meeting Beethoven, it would be highly improper and ungrateful to forget that he wrote nine symphonies and a whole lot of other magnificent music. You would not go to him and say, "I am honored to meet you, sir. I am grateful for your compositions, but of course we must not talk about that kind of thing now. You will want me to concentrate on our spiritual relationship." Beethoven would presumably be delighted to hear praise and appreciation of what he wrote. And we might reasonably expect that God will be glad to hear us talk gratefully about the good things of life that he has given us.

So love of God is distinguished, not by cancelling out all earthly loves, but by gathering them together and offering them up in praise and gratitude—and in prayer that they may be enjoyed without selfishness. God's people in Old Testament days seem to have understood this. An awful lot of the praise of God recorded in the Old Testament expresses delight in God's works and gratitude for them. Think of the *Benedicite,* an outburst of exhilarating praise, cataloguing all the good things in the created world. There is a saying that we use with particular emphasis: "You can put that in your pipe and smoke it!" It's a fine expression for clinching an argument, stuffing a truth down someone's throat, and telling him to swallow it. The Irish, however, have another expression for the same purpose, and it is most colorful: "You can set that to music and sing it!"

In Old Testament days God's people were always setting to music and singing their delight in the world they lived in, and everything in it that satisfied their senses and their minds. Surely this must be what God wants of us. He must want the full man, with all his faculties and responses, to thank him and worship him. He does not want a company of wraith-like phantoms who have temporarily sloughed off their pulsing humanity as they turn their thoughts from earthly ends to heavenly ends. One thing is certain. If you can't appreciate the earth, you've not going to appreciate heaven. Perhaps you're not even going to have the chance.

Loving the God who made us, with rejoicing in his created work, is of course only one side of the coin of worship. We must also love the God who saved us, with gratitude for his redemptive work. In this respect our love of God involves gratitude of a different kind from gratitude for the good things of earthly life. When you thank God for food and drink, sunshine and scenery, it can have something in common with thanking a man for the statue he has carved or the picture he has painted. You thank him with unmitigated joy, believing that, though he worked hard at what he made, he did so with delight and experienced a glad sense of achievement. But you cannot thank God for Jesus' saving death on the cross in exactly that spirit. If your daughter had been all but drowned at sea and rescued by a young man who lost his own life in the act, and you and she had to visit his young widow to express your appreciation and your "gratitude," the meeting would be solemn, the emotion heartfelt, and words used grave, measured, and empty of ebullience or exhilaration.

Love of God is fuelled by joyful gratitude for the creation and solemn gratitude for the Cross. Christian worship, corporate or individual, must express both forms of gratitude. Richard Baxter, the seventeenth-century English divine, got the balance perfect in his magnificent prayer of thanksgiving: "We bless thee for our creation, preservation, and all the blessings of this life; but, above all, for thine inestimable love in the redemption of the world by our Lord Jesus Christ, for the means of grace, and for the hope of glory."

However paradoxical it may seem, Christians are bound to thank God for the sufferings of his Son. That is one reason why the sacrament of the Lord's Supper has been central in the Church's life throughout history. By the same paradox many Christians celebrate the resurrection of Christ on Easter Day in a service which commemorates his suffering. Indeed they celebrate the birth of our Lord on Christmas Day in a service which commemorates his death. T.S. Eliot, in his play *Murder in the Cathedral,* includes a Christmas Day sermon by Thomas Becket, delivered a few days before his martyrdom. "We celebrate at once the Birth of Our Lord and His Passion and Death upon the Cross." We have to "rejoice and mourn at once for the same reason," he adds.

The paradox cuts deeply. John Donne wrote a poem in 1608 to mark a special coincidence. In that year the date fixed in the Church's calendar for celebrating the angel's Annunciation to the Virgin Mary that she should be the mother of Christ happened to coincide with Good Friday. Birth and death are linked, as Donne pictures the Virgin Mary promised a son at the age of "scarce fifteen" and bereft of her son at the age of fifty. The bringing of these two extremes together shows that "death and conception in mankind is one." The Christian knows that death is the gateway to life. In the supreme act of love God made this plain, and human love of him must always be mindful of it.

TWENTY-TWO

Love of Others

ONE OF THE FIRMEST New Testament commandments is that we should love one another. More specifically we are told to love our neighbors as ourselves. And when our Lord was pressed about what this meant, he told the story of the good Samaritan who stopped on his journey to help a poor fellow who had been mugged and beaten up and left wounded at the roadside. As ambulances were not then available he had to clean and bandage the fellow's wounds himself and get him to a hotel where he could be booked in and looked after at the Samaritan's expense. The whole thing was a pretty laborious business, and it is interesting that our Lord should have chosen an event so messy and so arduous to illustrate what love is like in action.

For of course when the idea of loving one another is presented to us we tend to think of situations and events rather more picturesque and romantic than doing an impromptu nursing job on a street corner. "Love is an emotion," we say, "and human love is the most beautiful emotion of all." We picture two lovers locked in each other's arms or a young mother suckling her baby. "That's what I mean by human love," we say to ourselves. And we are quite right of course—provided that such notions do not exhaust our concept of human love. When the New Testament speaks of love, it does not generally set us purring over mental pictures of lovers kissing or of babies' faces nuzzled against their mothers' breast. It speaks of men laying down their lives for their friends.

We have said that there is no genuine human love or desire—

even the love of boats or perfume—that cannot be involved in grateful love of God. But love of God is one thing and love of our fellowmen is another thing. For, as the story of the good Samaritan shows, love for our fellows requires us to answer their urgent needs. That is a first priority of human love. But God has no needs at all, urgent or non-urgent, for us or anyone else to answer.

It was appropriate to relate, say, our love of music or of dancing to love of God, because our love of these things is a matter of enjoyment, appreciation, and gratitude. We are grateful receivers and cannot strictly make a direct return either to the symphony that delights us or to Beethoven who wrote it. It is true that we can applaud the orchestra and the conductor and maybe give a contribution to the Musicians' Benevolent Fund; but orchestra and conductor too are, like us, beneficiaries of Beethoven, grateful to him but unable to do anything for him personally.

There would, however, be something selfish in comparing love of music with love of a fellow-being. Even our best and most admired friends do not invite us simply to bask in what they have to offer in enjoyment, appreciation, and gratitude— and to express these feelings in an occasional round of applause. Our friends need our help—as neither God nor Beethoven does. Unless we are continually on the lookout for what we can do to answer their needs, we make a poor return for their friendship.

The reader may worry now lest I am saying that love of God is more like love of music than love of a friend. It is not. Love of God, like love of a friend, is personal. There is a living being in each case to whom we are bound. And just as our friend wants something of us, so God wants everything of us. But wanting is not needing. God can always do quite well without us. Sometimes our friends cannot. Without the love of the good Samaritan, the battered victim of robbery would have died.

It is this crucial fact of human need that distinguishes our love of one another from our love of God. And, if you look at it in the right way, you will see that we are enormously privileged to be called upon to answer the needs of others. For love which answers the needs of others is not like man's love of God but like God's love of man. In this respect again we are mini-creators, made in God's image. His love sustains the universe and answers our physical needs. His love redeems us and answers our spiritual needs. We are allowed to play our part under him in answering human need.

As Christians we have to be continually on our guard lest we fall into the habit of singing sweet hymns of thankfulness for the love of others and of praying for the gift of love for others and then of wrapping the whole subject of love in a romantic haze. The practice of love is often neither a romantic nor even an emotional matter. When a man is suffering from cancer, the love that he needs is the love that saws off his foot. Sentiment would be out of place in the operating theatre. It is a place of disinfected atmosphere, gloved hands, masked faces, suppressed feelings, terse commands, disciplined obedience; a place where brains concentrate and fingers work deftly. But it is the only place where human love can answer the heartfelt need of many a suffering invalid. If you offered a cancer patient, instead of the surgeon's knife, the ardent embraces of the loveliest nurse from hospital film-land, he would say, "If that is what love means, then it's no help to me at all. Take it away!"

The love shown by the good Samaritan is to some extent institutionalized for us today in our hospitals and health services. We have medical care supervised by professionals. And the more we love our dear ones, the firmer we shall be in insisting that they submit themselves to the regimens and disciplines, and if necessary to the surgery, which medical expertise advises. It is illuminating to reflect on the operation of love in the care of our bodies, for so often it involves treatments which we are loath to undergo. Who wants to have a piece cut out of his inside? Who wants to be told that he must never touch alcohol again? Who wants to lie every night on a board instead of on a sink-in mattress? Yet these are the impositions of true love. We know it from our own experience. Think what devoted wives have been saying to their husbands in numberless homes this very day. "No, I won't make you bacon and eggs for breakfast. They're no good for you at all with your heart condition. Remember what the doctor said." "No, no, you can't have a drink. I've been firmly instructed to forbid it. In fact I've thrown the last bottle away." "No, no, no, you must not eat that chocolate. Your sugar intake today has been far too high already."

"No, no, no," is spoken in the name of love. And some people would like to pretend that forbidding people to do what they feel like doing belongs to a past age of outmoded moral dogmatism, authoritarianism, and paternalism. I have just been reading a survey of some recent books of sex education (some of them indeed supposed to be specifically Christian), and they all seem to have a rooted objection to the practice of forbidding anything to the young "for their own good." In the view of these writers it appears that love could never say no.

We have seen what nonsense that is. True love may often say no. Everyone who has brought up children knows that answering another's needs does not always mean giving them what they *think* they need, what they want, in fact. And this presents us with the most difficult problem of all in the practice of human love. You perhaps know someone who gets quarrelsomely "across" with people mainly through the fact that his best efforts are so tainted with vanity and self-assertiveness that he "must have his own way," as they say, even when he is supposedly engaged in good works. You know that he has an inordinate love of admiration and holding the center of the stage. Do you help him best by kindness and flattery which keep him in a good mood, boost his self-confidence, and produce a ready smile, but which do nothing to induce him to see himelf more clearly? Or do you try gently to prick the bubble of his vanity and help him to see himself as others see him?

The point of this example is twofold. In the first place it shows that love is not always best expressed in smiles of approval and praise. In the second place it shows that love can be hard work, for the appropriate expression of it has to be worked out before you act, or your "kindness" to another may do him harm rather than good.

TWENTY-THREE

Prayer

WHEN THE SON OF GOD himself came to live on this earth it was clearly essential that people should have the chance to know who he was. So our Lord did not conceal the facts when he was pressed. "Who do *you* think that I am?" he asked Peter and when Peter replied, "Thou art the Christ, the Son of God," Jesus congratulated him on his insight. Moreover Jesus performed miracles which no human power could effect. He did not, however, do them in order to win converts but in order to give help which it was beyond human capacity to give. Five thousand people who had followed him far from home were fed from a single basket of food, disabled people who appealed to him were cured of their infirmities, and Lazarus was raised from the dead. Such acts made it apparent that here was someone who was master of nature, Lord of created beings and things. "What manner of man is this," it was naturally asked, "that even the winds and the sea obey him?"

But just as it was essential that there should be clear indication of our Lord's identity, it was also essential that there should be no compulsion about people's response to it. The story of Christ's temptation in the wilderness makes this point clearly. Our Lord had only to tour the country as a great Wonder-Worker, leaping from towers without scratching or bruising himself, and turning stones into loaves of bread, and people would have been spellbound with admiration. He could have taken them and their world over in God's name. But what place would human love of the Father and free obedience to him have had in the hearts of those who were simply mesmerised by indisputable evidence of divinity come to earth? This would not have been winning the hearts of men but forcibly conscripting them. Adam and Eve had freely sinned the human race into disobedience. The second Adam must love the human race freely back into obedience.

So the Son of God, for the most part, conducted himself as the Son of Man. Not exclusively, as we have seen, but commonly enough to make people's response to him, as God, a matter of free decision. He ate and drank, walked in the countryside and sailed on the sea, visited friends, attended the temple, and rode on an ass.

Since God on earth behaved as a man, it is logical to assume that God in heaven will behave like God. He did not much go in for recognizable divine masterstrokes when he walked the earth, and he will not much go in for recognizable interventions on earth now that he is in heaven.

When we pray to him, we pray to one who will not adopt the policy of compulsive wonder-working which our Lord rejected when Satan tempted him with it. When we pray we are likely to have to wait for the unfolding of his answer through the ordinary events of life. And we shall not necessarily understand immediately his way of responding. It may be part of his treatment of us that we have to be seemingly rebuffed in a request rather than satisfied straightaway.

I have had to get up from my desk in the last few minutes to shoo a cat away from the lawn outside. It lives next door. I do not dislike cats. In fact I am rather fond of them. And this cat may well be bewildered that I, who have sometimes been known to welcome it in our garden by stroking it, should today drive it off with fearsome shouts and hostile hand-claps. But in fact it was eating the breadcrumbs my wife had put out for the birds. Two jays were hovering about dejectedly. Since I sent the cat packing they have come down and eaten the crumbs. There is no injustice in this. The cat has a good home and is well fed. Moreover, when the jays get crumbs they are perhaps less likely to forage damagingly in the garden elsewhere. Thus I play the

God in relation to beings of a lower order, manipulating the lives of dumb creatures. In response the cat may think I've turned hostile and wonder on what malicious principle we put food in front of its nose that it is forbidden to taste. The watchful jays, on the other hand, may flatter themselves that their colorful plumage can generally win them preferential treatment and that a black cat is a rather plain and humdrum creature by comparison with themselves. I can conceive that both my rebuff to the cat and my kindness to the jays may be misinterpreted by the feline mind and the avian mind, such as they are.

God does not answer requests like an automatic slot machine. You cannot put the appropriate coinage of prayer in the slot above the piled-up goodies, pull out the chosen drawer underneath, and extract the packaged chocolate or sugared almonds. For one thing, you may think you want chocolate when in fact God knows you would be better off in health for having an orange instead—or for doing without either.

As God does not answer prayers automatically, so too he does not answer them with crude compulsive literalness. If you are really short of money to feed and clothe your family and you pray desperately for help, the one thing that will certainly not happen is that an angel will knock at your door and deliver a sack of dollar bills with God's compliments. It is not impossible of course that a representative of a charitable agency may call and ask what help you need, or a job vacancy may be brought to your notice that will solve the problem, or even an unexpected bequest may come your way. But in all these instances it will be possible for you to say, "Well, I *did* pray; but I suppose this help might have come anyway."

That is the point. An angel knocking at the door with a sack of cash and God's compliments is not an invitation to faith and trust and love, but a forcible conscription of your recognition. When Christ in the wilderness turned his back on Satan's temptation to mesmerise mankind with marvels, he turned his back on door-to-door divine delivery of items from the universal prayer-catalogue.

You have to take it on trust from Christ's own promise ("Ask, and ye shall receive") and from the assurance of numberless Christians that God does answer prayer and that the answer is recognizable when it comes but often very different from what was pictured in advance. It will be of such a kind that you will be able to say, "It's just a coincidence that I prayed for his recovery and that now he has indeed got better." It will at the same time be of such a kind that you will be able to say, "God has clearly answered my prayer."

God looks after us and our needs. But he does it in his own way. Jesus himself, as he saw suffering and death immediately ahead for him, prayed that the cup might pass from him—though he added, "Nevertheless not my will but thine be done." In immediate literal terms the prayer was rejected, for Christ was crucified. But the prayer was richly answered when God raised Christ from the dead.

So when prayer seems difficult and we wonder whether we are being listened to or whether we are talking to ourselves, we need to ask the question, "What do I expect?" Do I expect, having prayed for my mother's recovery, to hear a divine voice saying, "Yes, certainly, I'll attend to it straightaway"? Do I expect to see her running downstairs and calling for her golf-clubs? And do I expect, having prayed that my cantankerous neighbor will cease to be so hostile, to find her knocking at my door forthwith, a sweet smile on her face and a bunch of flowers in her hand?

It is when we press the question: How could it be otherwise? that we recognize how exactly right is God's treatment of us.

TWENTY-FOUR

The Church

THERE USED TO BE A HABIT in the eighteenth century of referring to Jesus Christ as the "Founder of Christianity." Up to a point it is a just and harmless expression. But we tend to think of founders of movements as historic figures who did their work and then went their way. Lord Baden Powell was founder of the Scout movement and is still revered as such. Mary Baker Eddy founded the First Christian Science church and left the bulk of her fortune for the future extension of its work. But the Bible and Christian hymns speak of Christ, not as the founder of the Christian Church, but as the foundation-stone or corner-stone of the Christian Church. There is a difference between a founder and a foundation-stone. The founder does his work and goes on his way. If he has established a new society or built a new art gallery, he rejoices in the thought of what will outlive him. But the foundation-stone stays where it is. Take it away and the building collapses; there is nothing to outlast it.

Any founder of a human movement or society will be concerned about its future after his death. He may retire early as leader in order to ensure that his successor is to his liking. He wants to make sure that, after his death, the movement will continue to serve the principles on which he first conceived it. One can imagine with what care and anxiety the founder of a society will discuss with his closest subordinates the ways of guaranteeing its health and continuance after his death. He foresees his final separation from the society as a point of possible threat to its integrity.

111

The peculiar thing about Jesus' foundation of the Church was his insistence that he was not really going to leave it at all. In the first place he promised his disciples that, after his departure from the earthly scene, a "Comforter" would come to them, sent by the Father in his name. "But the Comforter, which is the Holy Ghost, whom the Father will send in my name, he shall teach you all things, and bring all things to your remembrance." How different this was from saying, "Now you must be sure that you stick firmly to the principles I have taught you." Such a warning was apparently unnecessary. "The Holy Spirit will come, tell you everything you need to know, and jolly your memories when necessary." In the second place, lest there should be any mistake about his relationship to the Holy Spirit, the promised Comforter, Jesus told them, "Lo, I am with you always even unto the end of the world."

So instead of a founder who gives instructions to his followers and goes his way, we have a Founder who assures them of continuing trustworthy guidance and of his continuing presence with them.

There are even more remarkable aspects of the society which Christ founded. Its members are not just people who pay their subscription fee, sign on the dotted line, receive their membership card, collect their copy of the rule-book, and do what they can to introduce others to the aims of the founder. For the Founder did not say to the disciples, "The Sermon on the Mount contains the essence of my teaching. Learn it by heart if you can, and print it in the rule-book for all new members to accept and to live by." Instead he said, "I am the Vine, ye are the branches." "I am the true Vine, and my Father is the husbandman." What sort of advice was this? "The heavenly Gardener will cut away the rotten branches and prune the fruitful ones. Grow in me and I will grow in you. If you live your life in me and my teaching lives in your hearts, then you can ask for what you want, and you will get it."

There is an extraordinary confidence here. The founder prepares to leave the earthly scene. Probably death is in prospect. His work has reached the stage of binding a dozen disciples—one of them unreliable—in the fellowship of leadership. They will go out and carry the message across the world. And there is nothing on the lines of preparing them practically for future contingencies; there is only the warning that they will be hated and persecuted, and the assurance that he will be continuingly with them.

So you join the Church, not in order to have your name appended to the list of adherents faithfully keeping the rules of the Founder. You join the Church in order to have your life grafted into the Founder's life. The Founder is alive in the members of the Church as the vine is alive in its branches. Indeed the Founder *is* the Church: its members are incorporated into the life of the Founder. "Founder" is no word to go on using. For no other religious leader has ever made the claim that Christ made: that he would live always in his members and they would live in him; that they are incorporated into his own body and that the continuing Church is indeed his continuing Body on earth.

We do not wish to press here definitions of the nature of the Church which divide Christians, sometimes deeply. But there can be no balking the truth that to be incorporated into the living Body of Christ is an awesome and fearsome as well as an exhilarating and heartening matter. It is awesome because of the gap between Christ's goodness and our sinfulness. It is fearsome because Christ foresaw hatred and persecution for his followers. It is exhilarating because he offers forgiveness of our sins through membership of his Body. It is heartening because he promised us the continuing grace of the Holy Spirit.

Either we live in Christ or our membership of the Church is of no effect. And we cannot live in Christ without sharing, to however small an extent, the pattern of experience which led to crucifixion. That share may, mercifully, be light. Not everyone is called upon to have nails driven through his flesh. But we all have to die, and to that extent, sooner or later, we shall learn more intimately what crucifixion involves.

On how far it is just to press the parallel between Christ's redeeming work and the experience of the Church Christians differ. There are those who, rightly conscious of the terrible either/or which God's call involves, insist that salvation is granted only to people who have responded individually, voluntarily, and decisively to Christ's words, "He who is not with me is against me." There are those who would say that, just as our Lord's self-sacrifice on the cross atoned for human sin and opened up the way of salvation, so the continuing worship and obedience of his present earthly Body, the Church, may somehow fill out for others the work of redemption.

What all mainstream Christians insist on is that membership in the Church is not an optional extra. You may decide to abstain from all alcoholic drink without joining a teetotal society, and you would have the right to tell any member of such a society, "I am as much a teetotaller as you are." There is no sense in which you could decide to keep the "Christian" rules without joining the Church and then claim, "I am as much a Christian as any Church member is." You are not. Biblical teaching is unambiguous on this point. To become a Christian is to become incorporated into the still-living Body of Christ. No amount of rule-keeping will so incorporate you. Only Baptism can effect the incorporation.

TWENTY-FIVE

Suffering

W E HAVE ALL COME ACROSS PEOPLE who don't know when to stop talking. We have all been visited at some time by a man who tells anecdote after anecdote from his past, chuckling away with the supposed fun of it all, while the faces of those who listen grow longer and longer. Eventually their eyes become glazed and even the mechanism of the politely smiling lips freezes. And afterwards we say to each other, "If only John knew what he sounded like! If only he could stop and listen to himself, he would learn what a bore he is."

The writer too needs to check up on what he is saying and what it all sounds like to the reader. Especially when he presumes to head a section of his book with a title like "Suffering." The reader may well mutter, "What does *he* know about it?" Indeed. I have just written in the previous section that we cannot live in Christ without sharing somewhere along the line in the kind of suffering that culminated in death on the cross. The reader may well wonder how genuine and heartfelt that statement is.

Well, I wonder myself. To begin with I have been writing these last few sections on beautiful spring days, days that have brought wonderful hours of sunshine after a hard winter. And I can look out of my study window and stare at Skiddaw, a three-thousand-foot mountain that changes color with the seasons. It can be white with snow, golden with dead bracken, purple with heather, pink or red in the evening sun. It's not exactly penal servitude to sit here and write in the mornings.

Especially since, after lunch, I shall take some exercise and probably walk in the continuing sunshine along the shore of Lake Derwentwater whose surrounds perhaps represent the loveliest square miles in our country.

So is there not something rather hypocritical about sitting here and telling other people that they must be prepared to suffer?

The question has become a pressing one because of two things that have happened this week. In the first place my publishers kindly sent me a pre-publication copy of Charles Turner's moving book, *The Celebrant*. It reconstructs, with fictional elaboration, the actual story of a young priest who felt a strong vocation to very special service to God and voluntarily insisted on going to minister to the dying in Memphis, Tennessee, when it was stricken by a plague of yellow fever in 1878. The priest could talk of Christ's suffering and self-sacrifice to the desperately afflicted without the risk of any possible comeback such as the reader might make to me: "Who are you to talk about suffering and self-sacrifice?" He practiced what he preached. And reading his story naturally made me wonder whether I had any right at all to continue writing a book that contains pious statements about the Christian having to bear his cross.

Then yesterday I heard news of a farmer hereabouts whose son, aged eighteen, hitherto apparently a normal healthy young man, was whisked into hospital a few weeks ago and has now died of leukemia. He has died of leukemia at eighteen and I am healthy in my sixties. The farmer has lost his son. My sons are all alive and well. None of this would seem to be relevant were it not that *I* am the fellow yapping on about suffering.

I strolled in the garden this morning before sitting down to write this section. And the thoughts I have just put down went through my head. But then another answering voice said something like this: "You're working yourself up into a grand melodramatic pose. You're beginning to picture yourself as a lily-white hero who is so pure in heart and single in mind that he can't write about the Christian vocation to share Christ's suffering because he's feeling cheerful in the spring sunshine and hasn't even got a headache. You're going to be the noble fellow who casts down his pen with a heroic gesture and declares, 'I am not worthy to write another sentence.' Come off it!"

None of us is worthy to preach the gospel we are called to preach. The mistake I was in danger of making a few moments ago was the mistake of imagining that I could possibly teach anything at all on *my* authority. Every word we utter in the name of Christ is spoken on *his* authority. It isn't *me* who is telling you that Christians have to bear their cross; it is God's truth set out in the Bible and repeated by every genuine Christian teacher since the Church was founded. So we'd better have no nonsense about my not being personally fitted to talk about this particular aspect of Christian truth. Otherwise I should be virtually claiming that I *am* personally fitted to talk about other aspects of Christian truth.

This, however, is not the whole answer to the question I have raised. When suffering people appealed to our Lord, he did not deliver little homilies to them about the necessity to bear pain with resignation. He cured them. He lifted the burden. He no more wanted a humanity tormented with physical and mental suffering than you and I do.

Moreover, although Christ's earthly sufferings can never be exaggerated, we must remember that the New Testament fastens on the Passion narrative with a magnifying glass. The events of the few days leading up to the crucifixion are recorded in increasingly intense detail until the final hours of agony. But even in a short life of thirty years there was time for a great deal of joy and sheer healthy living through the long decades prior to that last week. We do not hear that our Lord himself suffered from illnesses, minor physical ailments, or chronic distresses such as St. Paul had to put up with. Of course he knew what it was to lose friends by bereavement. He also knew what it was to keep things going with a swing at a wedding party.

Surely it is appropriate to remind ourselves that in all those hidden years there must have been many thousand times when

Christ sat down at a table to enjoy a meal with his family and with his friends. There must have been delight in manual work, delight in study, delight in walking, delight in friendship, delight in conversation, as well as delight in food and drink. Of how many suppers was the Last Supper the last? How many suppers were there which were not overshadowed by the approach of arrest and death? How many suppers at which bread was eaten and wine drunk without any thought or talk of a broken body and spent blood?

We must not try to be holier than our Lord. We must not imagine that suffering has to become the norm of the Christian life. We must thank God for whatever days are given us from which it is absent. We must pray that whenever or however it comes to us, we shall be given strength to bear it. When the pain is real and not imaginary, when it is unmerited and not the consequence of self-indulgence, then will be the time to start linking our sufferings mentally with those of Christ. Until then it is advisable to see his sufferings in the eyes of others.

TWENTY-SIX

Joy

I OUGHT TO BE ABLE to write convincingly about joy this morning because the sun is shining even more brilliantly, though three weeks have passed since I wrote about suffering. It's the end of April. The day is warm. The fields are full of ewes and lambs. Wherever one walks there are lambs to watch. They skip about in their leggings, as the poet Andrew Young observed, "jumping over little hills that aren't there." It is true that it was temporarily saddening to hear last night of two ladies hereabouts who have to go into hospital for masectomies. But since both of them are over seventy years old, reason observes that either might have had to face a worse diagnosis. There are other reminders of grimmer realities elsewhere. Last night's news bulletin described a British naval landing on South Georgia, and hostilities seem likely to extend to the Falkland Islands.

On any morning, if we were to cast up a balance-sheet of good news and bad news, personal and local, public and far-reaching, we might wonder whether it was our duty to smile or to be grave. But in fact the Bible instructs us to rejoice. It is a repeated biblical command. "Rejoice and be exceeding glad, for great is your reward in heaven." "Rejoice in the Lord alway, and again I say rejoice." The rejoicing, we observe is rooted in the Lord and is related to a heavenly reward. Nevertheless the biblical exhortation is firm. And there are no biblical instructions to us to be miserable—except about our sins.

We are to rejoice in the Lord. That is sensible enough. You can't just rejoice. You have to rejoice over *something*. That is the

119

crucial thing about all happiness. When you are really deliriously happy, you don't say to yourself, "How happy I am!" You are too busy with other thoughts, such as, "How magnificent is the view from this mountaintop!" or "How beautiful is this girl in my arms!" or "How tremendous is this symphonic climax!"

Now it is true that the New Testament warns us that we shall suffer. But a warning is one thing, and a command is another thing. Yes, we shall suffer, but we are commanded to rejoice— even in suffering. Little as we may be able to digest this, we can at least recognize that suffering is not the opposite of joy, because we ourselves have received cheerful smiles from beds of pain. No, suffering is not the opposite of joy. Misery is the opposite of joy. Heroic people can be joyful in suffering, it seems, but no one can be joyful in misery. There is a certain kind of person of whom we say, "He seems to enjoy being miserable," but we are conscious of paradox and exaggeration in speaking thus. We know that at any given moment either misery or joy must be paramount. They cannot coexist simultaneously.

Joy is about something. And misery? Is it not really about nothing? You may say that it is all about the lack of joy, the lack of health, the lack of money, the lack of comfort, the lack of prestige, and so on. But no "lack" can make a something. Misery is essentially about nothing. Joy is always about something.

Surely that is what we should expect after our examination of the difference between good and evil. Good is positive, substantial: evil is negative; it is deficiency. Evil is absence of the good and perversion of the good.

That is why, in the long run, heaven is the only endurable final condition for mankind: because hell is not a condition but a deprivation of condition, not a place but a deprivation of place, not an experience but a deprivation of experience. Hell is a desperate, because hopeless, yearning for *something* from the depths of negation and loss.

The message of the New Testament is that we must live in

Christ. And of the various events in the chronicle of Christ's doings the later things are no less important than the earlier things. We must live in Christ, the Christ who taught and healed, who called people to repentance and promised everlasting life, who suffered at the hands of ungodly people and surrendered his life on the cross. We must live in Christ, and the cross was not the end of Christ. He was raised from the dead. His resurrected body walked the earth, and finally his resurrected body was taken from men's sight and ascended into heaven.

We say this, if we are Christians. We repeat it in our creeds. We believe it. But do we allow these tremendous truths to color all our thinking? Do we picture ourselves as future resurrected bodies being taken up into heaven? Are we not rather inclined to treat the resurrection and ascension of Christ as some kind of symbolic guarantee for us of life hereafter in a vaguely conceived disembodied state?

Let us recall what did *not* happen after Christ's death on the cross. There was no sorrowful gathering of mournful disciples in the upper room at which suddenly a mysterious voice was about their ears, saying, "I am Jesus. I died on the cross. My body lies in the tomb. But do not continue to grieve for me, for as you can hear I am still alive. My body may rot in the tomb. But in the spirit I live on. And you too will share this immortality of the soul. You too, when your bodies die, will become disembodied spirits freed from the clogging flesh, to dwell forever in an eternity of spiritual joy and light."

Why did not Jesus act like this? Was it just that God could not trust men to believe in a disembodied voice? Was it just that, in the days before the tape-recorder, purely aural evidence was inadequate to convert doubt into faith?

No. God gave men the solid evidence of a human body resurrected because that was what he meant human bodies to be. They were to be resurrected. Of course the God who, through Christ, healed the lame and the blind, was not the kind of God to confer instant immortality on the deformed and the crippled just as they are. He is a healing God as well as a resurrecting God. But likewise the God who raised the crucified body from the tomb was not the kind of God to write off the experience of flesh and blood as a prelude to some kind of vaporously nebulous status. We are not due to become disembodied voices floating in infinitude. There was no seance in the upper room, no table-tapping, no ectoplasmic phantom, no third-party contacts between a world of spirit and a world of matter. Instead, Jesus himself stood in the midst of them, and invited Thomas to take a closer look at the wounded hands and the wounded side.

A body like ours, having died, was raised from the dead, and having been raised, was taken up into heaven. That is the Christian teaching. That and the assurance that Christ's experience is to be ours also. No wonder the New Testament bids us rejoice. For all the joys we know of are connected with the senses, the mind, and the imagination, which the human physique embodies, and if all this is to be eternally alive in heaven, uplifted and transfigured, then the promise of heaven is something we can barely entertain for a second without a thrill of almost unbearable delight. No wonder that majestic scene from the mountaintop inspired you, no wonder that beautiful body in your arms delighted you, and no wonder that tremendous musical climax excited you: for these were each and all foretastes of what a closer experience of God's splendor and magnificence will one day convey.

That is what the hope of heaven means. And it is not an optional extra in Christian belief. It is basic and essential to God's promise to man made known in the living Christ. There is no irony in the command to rejoice.

TWENTY-SEVEN

Worship

WE HAVE CONSIDERED the kind of prayer in which we appeal to God on our own behalf (which is called "petition") or on behalf of others (which is called "intercession"), but we have said little yet about the purely disinterested prayer of praise. It is, in fact, one of the most difficult things to talk about precisely because it is disinterested—because it can produce no measurable results in earthly terms. A petitionary prayer is designed to produce a healed body, a penitential prayer is designed to produce a healed soul—but what is an act of praise intended to produce?

"To offer praise to God, then, is the primary activity and function of the Christian Church," writes E.L. Mascall in his fine little book *Grace and Glory*. The primary activity and function of the Church. Does that take a bit of swallowing? Not if one thinks carefully about it. The primary thing is always distinguishable from secondary things; but there could be no primary thing unless there were secondary things, and praise or worship would not be the primary duty if no other duties accompanied it in the way of carrying out the commands of the one we worship: to heal the sick, to tend the fatherless and widows, to minister to the poor and the afflicted. Without these activities worship would not be the primary activity: it would be the sole and isolated activity.

Now one of the difficulties in talking about worship of God is that it is dead easy for anyone to ridicule worship by assuming a supposed God's-eye view which is in fact just an inflated man's-eye view. You know the kind of argumentative banter this attitude produces. "Whatever sort of God is this? Does he sit on a throne toting up the numbers of human beings who are on their knees in worship Sunday by Sunday? Does the angelic bureaucracy log the annual qualitative and quantitative output of mortal praise? And is this record kept on some vast spiritual computer that can register the latest human worship ratings in response to the tap of an angelic finger or the flip of an angelic wing; or are they still relying up there on steam-age random sampling or controlled selective sampling for keeping their praise-charts up to date?"

We have all read ridicule of the smug deity who sits with his head thrown back sniffing up the incense of worship from millions of human hearts and turning up the multiphonic volume-control to relish the amplified chorus of hymn-singing voices.

Yet praise of God is "the primary activity and function of the Christian Church." And, if you study your Bible, you may well begin to wonder, not whether today we are especially sensitive to the absurdity of pure worship, but whether we are today especially insensitive to the importance of true worship. Have we gained an insight or lost a faculty?

Consider the psalms. Whatever else may be said of them, one thing is clear: they are the record of a people who could not keep quiet about the glory and majesty of God. They are so uninhibited in this respect that by comparison they make much of the material of modern worship sound insipid, spineless, and arid—the languid, squeamish utterance of thin-lipped, repressed semi-paralytics. "Great is the Lord and highly to be praised in the city of our God and even upon his holy hill." "O Lord how wonderful are thy works." "Praise the Lord, O my soul, and all that is within me praise his holy name." Jubilant outbursts of this kind are scattered all over the psalms. They throb with the excitement of pure worship—of hearts which are asking for nothing but simply giving praise.

It is very difficult for us today to recapture this zest of pure worship. One reason why it is difficult is that we seek to justify everything we do by tangible results for ourselves or others. We hear a church service praised because it "made me feel good." Acts of worship are turned into experiences of emotional togetherness which are valued for the personal boost they provide for individuals and groups. But anything which twists the purpose of worship back into conscious self-improvement is alien to that bouncing outgoingness represented by the psalmist's shouts of delight in the hill of Sion, the city of our God, the Lord our Governor, great in Sion and high above all people.

E.L. Mascall has pointed out in *Grace and Glory* that praise takes the self-centeredness out of love. We have already shown how happiness is always directed away from the self to the source of joy: the beautiful view, the beautiful beloved, the beautiful symphony, or the beautiful picture. That is the nature of joy. And worship is joy turned backwards towards God—the source of all joy. For whatever it is that gives one happiness, God is its ultimate source. It is quite right to express gratitude to the orchestral players and the conductor after a moving performance of a symphony. A little reflection reminds us that we must feel gratitude to Beethoven too. And a little further reflection reminds us that we must show gratitude to the God who gave us Beethoven and who made the human brains and skills that conceived and manufactured violins and trumpets.

If the psalmists of the Old Testament felt the compulsive urge to praise God, how much more ought we to feel it. Those ebullient cries of admiration for God's majesty and loving-kindness came before God's Son was sent to earth to die for us, to win forgiveness for us, to show the way to everlasting life. They came before the blind and crippled had been healed at his touch, before he had formed the apostolic company which was to carry the gospel across the world, before the body and blood were given in bread and wine at the Last Supper or in sweat and agony on the cross. Those psalmists' shouts of delight in God's unfailing mercy came before the Son of God was raised from the dead, before the Holy Spirit was promised and descended among us.

It is not surprising that forms of worship, since the Church was founded, have tended to focus on the saving acts of redemption, on the Christ of the Last Supper, the cross, and the resurrection. If the Old Testament psalmist had cause for rapturous paeans of praise, what about us of later centuries who have seen the work of salvation completed?

There is a sense in which praise is self-proliferating. This section devoted to it shows that it is. You cannot investigate the motive of worship, the purpose of worship, and the meaning of worship without discovering that man is drenched in a flood of God-given blessings which would seem to call him to throw himself prostrate before God in gratitude and adoration.

At this point someone may protest: "How smug and complacent can you get? Here is a fellow prating about worship, gratitude, and adoration. Has he no knowledge of the numbers of babies dying from starvation in the time it takes him to pen his flowery sentences? Has he no notion of the world's exploited millions, of bodies riddled with disease, of rat-ridden tenements and shacks that stink of pollution? Has he never seen fatal cases of hydrophobia or lockjaw, cancer of the lung or delirium tremens? Come off it! Talk about the real world."

There is only one reply to this. There was no evasion of stark human reality by those Old Testament psalmists who sang the praise of God. They knew all about the arrow that flieth by night and the sickness that destroyeth in the noonday. They knew all about grief and exile, oppression and starvation, wasting flesh and bones protruding through the skin. Nor was there any evasion of stark human reality by the Son of God, who was brutally lashed, nailed upon the gallows, and had a sword plunged into his side. If you want to attack religion for not facing the harshest realities of life, you will have to turn your attention away from mainstream Christianity.

TWENTY-EIGHT

Revelation

THERE HAS RECENTLY BEEN an interesting controversy in our
local newspaper about the proposal to build a new theater
in our little town, Keswick. Now Keswick has a small permanent population, but it is a flourishing tourist center with a
lively little theater in a temporary building that will not last
much longer. In the Lake District it is a good idea to provide
indoor amusements for summer holiday-makers who stand a
fair chance of having a few days washed out by drenching rain.
Controversy about the proposal to build a new and permanent
theater turns first on the question whether a theater is needed at
all, and then on such questions as where it should be sited, what
kind of building it should be, and what additional amenities
ought to be provided alongside it. Shall it be sited at the lakeside
with a cafe attached overlooking Derwentwater, or shall it be
placed on the now derelict site of the once busy railway station?
Shall it be part of a larger complex involving also a swimming
pool, or an even larger complex including a conference center?

This kind of controversy produces picturesque plans, idealistic conceptions, and excited arguments. It is a fascinating field
for enthusiastic discussion. And yet all the heated thinking and
talking relate to a hypothesis which some people believe will
surely materialize while others believe it will never come to
anything. It's the stuff of a real living future to some and of idle
dreams to others.

Controversy about a project that might or might not be

actualized: is not a good deal of human thought and talk about religion similar to this?

The question is asked because we have had a different kind of local controversy here in recent years. It has not concerned a theater which might or might not materialize, but a mountain, Skiddaw, which towers three thousand feet above Keswick. Some time back there was heated argument about where the new main road linking the London motorway with industrial West Cumbria should be laid. The mountain was the problem. Run the new road on the most obvious, economic, and convenient route and it takes heavy traffic through the heart of the lovely country around Bassenthwaite Lake, which tourists visit in search of peace and quiet. The only alternative to this was a costly new engineering project routing the new road a long, long way round on the further side of the mountain. This economically costly project was highly favored by environmentalists and was of course rejected. Skiddaw has also been the cause of other controversies. The Forestry people have been under fire for their policy of coating its flanks with geometrical rows of conifers by nature alien to the area. And recently some enterprising entrepreneur in the tourist trade suggested that a cable railway to carry visitors to the top of the mountain might prove a powerful new attraction to the area. Once again of course the preservationists were horrified.

Such are the controversies about the theater and the mountain. Note the differences between them. The controversies about the theater derive their force from the fact that there may or may not be a new theater, and its possible future character is something everyone can think about for himself. The controversies about the mountain derive their force from the fact that it is inescapably there, billions of tons of it, immovable, unshakable, and no one can plan anything in its environment without reckoning with it.

Now all controversy about Christianity is like controversy about the mountain. It is not like controversy about the theater.

This has perhaps of late been the most misunderstood aspect of the Christian faith. It is not a collection of speculations about what might be. It is a record of what is. The Christian is not engaged in constructing a philosophy of life. He is busy learning and interpreting what has happened. And what has happened is a matter of history recorded in the Old and New Testaments. That history, the tale of God's dealings with men, we call his revelation. For God made himself known to his chosen people through the patriarchs and prophets—and that is what the Old Testament is all about. And then he made himself finally and fully known to them through coming among them in the person of Jesus Christ—and that is what the New Testament is all about.

The Old and New Testaments are not collections of theories about what might be, but records of what is and has been. The whole Christian revelation they record, therefore, is like a mountainous mass running across the map of human history. No one can pretend that it isn't there. Everyone who is at all concerned with the meaning of life and the destiny of the human race will have to take it into account.

The old Greek philosophers constructed theories that could answer their demand to understand the meaning of life. Some of them reasoned in such a way that they proved for themselves the existence of God. In this manner they satisfied their hunger for rational explanation of the world they lived in. But the Old Testament writers did not attempt to prove that God existed any more than our local preservationists try to prove that Skiddaw exists. And for the same reason. He was a mountainous presence in their history and experience. The religious theories of the Greek philosophers, we said, answered their demand for meaning and satisfied their hunger for rational explanation of things—just as the projected Keswick theater answers the demands of the planners and will satisfy the hunger of the tourists for entertainment. The planners will do their best to make sure that the theater meets these needs as the Greek philosophers were at pains to construct a system of belief to meet human needs.

The faith of Christians is not something fabricated to satisfy human need and comfort human feelings. It certainly provides a rational explanation of the universe and of human destiny; but it does not do so in virtue of the fact that, by trial and error, by speculation and argument, human beings have gradually hammered out for themselves a creed just right for their inquiring minds and restless hearts. It provides a rational explanation of the universe and of human destiny because it is based on God's revelation to man.

Indeed, if you think about it seriously even for a few moments, you will realize that human brains could never have concocted on their own the system of belief which is represented by Christianity. We know well enough today what kind of a system of beliefs men and women will make for themselves if they are intent on answering their demands and satisfying their hungers. We have evidence all around us of humanly fabricated faiths that are supposedly designed to give purpose to life and make individuals happy. Psychologists and sociologists, mediamen and writers, make fortunes by peddling codes of self-centeredness and supposed self-fulfillment that pack our mental hospitals and our jails, deface our streets with violence and our homes with misery.

Christianity promises no theater to keep you comfortable on the stormy days: it deposits a mountain in front of you. As Dorothy Sayers said, "It is hopeless to offer Christianity as a vaguely idealistic aspiration of a simple and consoling kind; it is, on the contrary, a hard, tough, exacting, and complex doctrine, steeped in a drastic and uncompromising realism."

There is an attitude abroad today which looks to religion for a personal boost, whereas the Christian looks to it for a revealing of truth. Christianity is essentially a matter of historic truth, not a mere recipe for personal well-being. The modern obsession with finding "a faith to live by" implies that you need a religion to keep you confident as you need pills to send you to sleep or a car to get you to work in time. That is topsy-turvy. Finding a faith is not a clinical problem like curing your corns. For the crucial question is not "How can I live a fulfilled life?" but "How can I live as God wants me to live?"

The paradox evidenced by millions of Christians is that in

finding the right answer to the second question you also find the right answer to the first question. But only if you sweep the first question from your mind and concentrate on the second. It never works the other way around, for just as the Christian faith and the history of the Church is the public revelation of God to man, so every individual Christian life privately unfolds the revelation of God to man.

TWENTY-NINE

Hope

FAITH, HOPE, AND LOVE are sometimes called the three "theological virtues." It is useful to bear this expression in mind for there is a difference between them and other virtues. If a Christian and a non-Christian were discussing someone and it was said that he had great fortitude or courage, great honesty or patience, they would probably use these words, "fortitude," "courage," "honesty," and "patience," with full understanding of each other's meaning. What applies to these virtues also applies to the vices. If a Christian and a non-Christian were discussing someone and it was said that he was given to sloth or vanity, then they would likewise use these words, "sloth" and "vanity," with full understanding of each other's meaning. On the whole, virtues and vices are defined in words whose meaning is shared between believers and unbelievers. The Christian and the non-Christian would be unlikely to get into a fierce argument about what the word "courage" or "honesty" means. They might dispute whether Mr. X was really courageous or really honest, but they would probably have identical notions in their minds as to what constitutes being courageous or honest.

When we turn to the "theological virtues" we find that this is no longer the case; and therefore the definition, "theological" virtues, is a useful one. For a person who has no time for theology will plainly have little interest in something called "theological virtue" if that definition is a just and meaningful one. Such a person—a firm unbeliever—would be unlikely to use theological vocabulary much anyway (unless for purposes of ridicule). You would not hear him talking about "original sin" or the "incarnation." But the words, "faith," "hope," and "love" might be a familiar part of his vocabulary. "I have great faith in oil for investment purposes," he might say. "I hope that we shall see a Stock Market rally next week."

Plainly we are here somewhat remote from the biblical use of the words "faith" and "hope." Among the first verses of the Epistle of St. Peter are the ringing words, "Blessed be the God and Father of our Lord Jesus Christ, which according to his abundant mercy hath begotten us again unto a lively hope by the resurrection of Jesus Christ from the dead, to an inheritance incorruptible and undefiled and that fadeth not away, reserved in heaven for you." In the Old Testament God is our hope. In the New Testament Jesus Christ is our hope. And the Epistle to the Hebrews speaks of the "hope set before us" as "an anchor of the soul."

By faith in Christ and his resurrection we attain the hope of ultimate glory. That is the relationship between Christian faith and Christian hope. Neither is based on earthly goods or grounded in earthly prospects. Indeed we must note the paradox that faith and hope in material earthly prospects are likely to leave no room for Christian faith and hope. Conversely, the utter failure of earthly prospects may prove to be the breeding ground for Christian faith. Indeed Christian hope comes most surely and savingly into play when earthly hopes are dashed. In that sense, certainly, it is the anchor of the soul.

Not of course that all earthly hopes are to be despised. Far from it. There is a limited earthly future as well as an eternal heavenly future to foresee for every Christian. And if he prays that his arthritis will be cured, he hopes that God will cure it. If he prays that his wife will recover after her driving accident, he rightly hopes that his prayer will be answered exactly. But if these hopes are dashed he will not be hopeless, for that anchor of the soul remains firm, the hope begotten by Christ's resurrection which foresees an inheritance reserved in heaven that will never fade.

There are people of great ebullience who seem to exude optimism. They slap you on the back. They tell you to cheer up. They assure you that every cloud has a silver lining and that everything will turn out for the best in the long run. If they happen to be clergy they tend to infuse into every service they conduct a let's-all-be-jolly-together spirit. It is wrong to condemn cheerfulness. The New Testament tells us to rejoice. But, if you are like me, you may find the perpetual-cheerfulness-mongers rather trying. Their quips and chuckles—if they are much given to them—may even sadden you. Possibly this is very much a matter of individual temperament, an aspect of the fact that, fortunately, we human beings are not all of a pattern stamped out on a mass-production line, but immensely varied in personality and taste. But I for one would certainly want to make a clear distinction between optimism-boosting and Christian hope. I suspect that if I were in dire trouble, faced with a grave operation or threatened with a probable bereavement in the family, then the optimism-booster is the last person I should want to meet. I should want to be consoled, not by someone who refused to face the solemn realities of human sickness and mortality, but by someone who soberly measured the prospect of death and reminded me of that Christian hope which no earthly disaster ought to be able to destroy. This kind of hope is not expressed by saying, "Cheer up. She's on the mend, I think," when the sands of life are plainly running out. It does not try to banish all grief or to replace suffering by gaiety. It points the way through the experience of grief and suffering to the hope of eternal life.

It is never helpful to encourage people in trouble to cling to escapist dreams of a sudden turn in fortune. That kind of "hopefulness" is a snare. I have told elsewhere how C.S. Lewis pointed to the danger of encouraging such illusions by saying, "Hope is the fawning traitor of the heart." Clearly Lewis, though he wrote eloquently about Christian hope in *Mere*

Christianity and elsewhere, was very sensitive to the sharp distinction between delusive hope and Christian hope, between earthly optimism and confidence in an eternal future. The one kind of hope may be the heart's treachery. The other is the soul's anchor.

THIRTY

The Christian Inheritance

A PREDOMINANT THEME in our reflections throughout this book has been the need to take a "big" view. The Christian looks at life, not just in terms of material immediacies (How can I pay the rent this month as well as that bill for car repairs?), but in terms of the progress from the cradle to the grave (What am I supposed to be doing here anyway, "crawling between earth and heaven"—as Hamlet put it?). There are perhaps two major obstacles to Christian conversion in our day, selfishness and small-mindedness. On the whole we do not want to have our own daily concerns with immediate matters—food and drink, home and comfort, money and career, pleasure and entertainment—disturbed or questioned. In the first place we do not want these priorities questioned because probing the motives that sustain them will bring our selfishness to light. In the second place we do not want to open our minds to the larger issues. We are too small-minded readily to conceive of our individual course from day to day within the context of the sweep of human life from birth to death and the sweep of human history from creation to its culmination.

It could be plausibly argued that today, more perhaps than in any previous age, we have become too small-minded to be Christians. Our vision is too narrow, our outlook too limited for us to be able to live familiarly with the great insights of Christendom which see human history held in the hands of God and the human race acting out through the centuries the drama that began with Creation, reached its turning point in the

137

Incarnation and Crucifixion, and will have its denouement in Heaven. We have all met men and women whose intelligence is minimal but who nevertheless seem to be able to jog through life in tolerable contentment. We say of them, "Fortunately he is too dim to know how dim he is." It can be argued that our century has now produced generations of men and women who are too small-minded to be aware of their own small-mindedness. This small-mindedness can be attributed to various causes. One, no doubt, is the prevalence in our environment of influences which pull down the shutters on perspectives that reach beyond the immediate. The press and television are influences of this kind. They pin our attention feverishly on getting and spending in our individual lives. And they focus on public affairs largely insofar as those passions for individual getting and spending are inflated into collective political rivalries on the national scene and ideological rivalries on the international scene. Another cause of our current small-mindedness is the prevailing notion of individual well-being spread by psychologists and sociologists, teachers and politicians. It fastens on the supposed need of the self for unfettered self-expression and self-fulfillment in isolation from the great bonds and obligations which draw the human family together across the continents and even across the centuries.

We spoke in the first section of this book of how men and women today try to turn religion into something like a personal attribute or possession, speaking of loss of faith as a clinical misfortune like varicose veins. Such thinking is characteristic of our age. There are distinguished twentieth-century writers who have regretted in print their misfortune in having to live in an age of lost values and collapsed belief. This is surely a blinkered, narrow-minded, and self-centered attitude. "Pity poor me now that the Christian Faith is discredited. How deep is my agony now that modern knowledge has exploded Christian credentials. Sympathize with my misery. Drop a tear for my searching soul, shorn of comfort and hope!"

Surely, surely, what is most disturbing about any thought that the Christian Faith might not be true is not *my* predicament but the world's predicament, humanity's predicament. Ponder the thought. Weigh its implications. That this vast age-long experience of millions of Christians through the centuries has been based on a fraud. That it is one huge product of human self-deception. That the whole body of human thought and the whole totality of human action recorded in the Bible and involved in the production, circulation, and study of the Bible should have been a gigantic waste of time. That the immense mass of human inspiration and toil and energy involved in the building of cathedrals and churches and in the construction of great masterpieces like the *Divine Comedy, Paradise Lost,* the *B Minor Mass,* or Leonardo's *Last Supper* should have been a colossal blunder. The thought that you or I might have got things all wrong does not, after all, strike at the roots of anything very significant in the history of the universe and the experience of mankind. But the thought that Peter and Paul and the apostles, Augustine and Aquinas and Luther and all the great Christian scholars, Dante and Milton and all the great Christian writers, Francis and Teresa and all the millions of saintly and less saintly men and women who have enriched human life by works of mercy and works of culture—the thought that all these should have been acting under an unspeakably erroneous delusion seems to be staggeringly incredible. Myself, I'm too skeptical to concede that possibility. Far too skeptical to be, in the shallow modern sense, skeptical.

Now this particular source of strength for the Christian is a special bonus. It was not there for the early disciples. It was not available for them. They could not turn to each other or to the uncommitted and say—as I have been saying here—"How can the gospel be false when all these past centuries of Christian sanctity and Christian achievement behind us testify to its strength and lastingness?" The early disciples had their own wonderful advantages of course in their close proximity to our Lord or to direct witnesses of our Lord. And one must never suggest that the objective record of Christian witness and achievement can be measured in the same scale as the living faith of unqualified personal commitment to our Lord. But there is every reason today to cultivate an alert awareness of our historic Christian inheritance, our fellowship with the community of those who have gone before us and are alive still in Christ. That community includes the simple and the unlettered, and it includes the gifted, the wise, and the scholarly. It includes men and women of all diversity of talents who have left the marks of Christian commitment and Christian understanding, not only in missionary activity, in the network of worshipping communities scattered over the globe, but also in works of scholarship, works of art, works of civic and cultural enterprise; in schools, colleges, hospitals, homes; all of which testify to the comprehensiveness of the Christian understanding and the objective solidity of Christian achievement.

The linkage which unites Christians in a common body is a linkage which crosses the boundaries of the centuries as well as the lines of longitude and latitude. We spoke of the Christian revelation as a vast mountain deposited across the map of history. The Christian community, the Church, is a massive body spread out across the map of history. It is a body quivering with life in all its members. *All* its members; not just those passing here and now between birth and death. That is the community the Christian joins at Baptism.

Printed in the United States
125896LV00002B/22/A

9 781573 833127